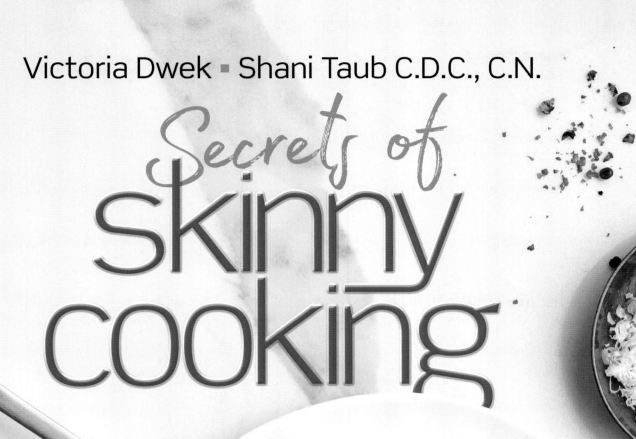

Victoria Dwek ▪ Shani Taub C.D.C., C.N.

Secrets of
skinny
cooking

Mouthwatering
Recipes
You Won't Believe
Are Low Calorie

Photos and
Styling by
Esti Photography

Published by **ARTSCROLL / SHAAR PRESS**
4401 Second Avenue / Brooklyn, NY 11232 / (718) 921-9000 / www.artscroll.com

Distributed in Israel by **SIFRIATI / A. GITLER**
POB 2351 / Bnei Brak 51122 / Israel / 03-579-8187

Distributed in Europe by **LEHMANNS**
Unit E, Viking Business Park, Rolling Mill Road
Jarrow, Tyne and Wear, NE32 3DP / England

Distributed in Australia and New Zealand by **GOLDS WORLD OF JUDAICA**
3-13 William Street / Balaclava, Melbourne 3183, Victoria / Australia

Distributed in South Africa by **KOLLEL BOOKSHOP**
Northfield Centre / 17 Northfield Avenue /
Glenhazel 2192, Johannesburg, South Africa

ISBN-10: 1-4226-1898-6 / ISBN-13: 978-1-4226-1898-1

Printed in Canada

Sabich Salad
(page 142)

With Thanks To...

Be careful with your
berachos rishonos and *acharonos*
[blessings made before and after eating].
When we thank Hashem for the food,
we also become conscious of
what we're eating. The *rishonah*
helps us know exactly what
we are putting into our
mouths instead of eating
mindlessly. When we say
the *acharonah*, we're
thankful, we're satiated ...
and we're done!

–Shani

Hashem, the Source of all our strength, Who has given us this tremendous opportunity. We sincerely hope that You gift us with the merit to help others gain happiness and feel good about themselves through this book.

My **mother and siblings,** for constantly helping me throughout my childhood and through the experiences that brought me to my current profession. To my **husband and children**, for always helping and supporting me in my career. And to my **mother-in-law**, for always accommodating me with healthy foods and helping me brainstorm new healthy recipe ideas. –Shani

No one realizes that when there's trial and error, someone still has to eat the "errors." Thank you to my **husband and children** for tasting 30 batches of corn muffins (and many more experiments). The testing is done. I promise to now only make your favorites. To my **mother** and **mother-in-law**, I'm so lucky to have your strong support system. –Victoria

To **Leah Schapira**, for starting me off on this cookbook journey, and always being a mentor and friend. You're the invaluable "wall" I bounce things off, throughout this project and all others … (even if you prefer to cook with a bit more oil). –Victoria

Dish by dish, we watched **Esti Waldman of Esti Photography** bring the scenes of this book alive through food styling and photography. We're so lucky to be the beneficiaries of your creativity and professionalism.

"Do you want to manage the food pages?" Thank you to **Rechy Frankfurter** of *Ami Magazine* for asking me that question seven years ago. It's been an exciting journey. –Victoria

Verdini Greens @VerdiniGreens for the pretty greens that top the dishes and **House of Granite and Marble** @HouseofGraniteandMarble for the beautiful stone that goes under the plates.

The ArtScroll Team

Thank you again to the publishers, **Rabbi Meir Zlotowitz** and **Gedaliah Zlotowitz**, for the opportunity and your confidence.

To the editor, **Felice Eisner**, our most valuable eyes, and our partner in making this the best it can be. It's always a pleasure to collaborate with you.

Graphic designer **Devorah Cohen** listened to the vision of the book and executed a design to match. Thank you for lending your talent, from start to finish.

To **Eli Kroen**, for adding his genius to the cover design.

To **Tova Ovits** and **Judi Dick**, for ensuring the book is perfect yet again.

Table of Contents

Dairy
creamy, cheesy & all you really want

Chicken & Meat
make mains exciting again

Fish
the light, feel-good main dish

Desserts
and sweet & salty treats

To My Readers

*O*f all the books I've worked on, this is the one I dreamed about writing for the longest time. Because this is the one that could actually help people.

There's lots of delicious food out there. Plenty of recipes with fat and sugar that taste really, really good. I think we all know that.

But I realized that what people didn't know ... is that light food can be just as satisfying.

It always pained me to see people struggle or express their feelings of deprivation when dieting (or frustration with not being able to).

I once overheard a man remark, "It's so hard not to have cake and donuts every day."

I remember feeling shocked. Cake? Donuts? Every day?

I knew that life doesn't have to be cake-less or donut-less (and most definitely not ice cream-less). But every day?

But it's no wonder he was missing his usual fare. On his diet, he was eating plain tuna every single day for lunch.

I'd visit friends and see them pull their diet dinners out of the oven. Plain roast chicken, dusted with paprika. Plain green beans and plain brown rice, all cooked in a 9- x 13-inch pan. Those pans looked so depressing and tasteless. No wonder most people don't stay on those regimens for long.

But what if everyone knew that they could enjoy — really enjoy — low-calorie meals just as much as any other food?

They could be healthy; they could feel good about themselves and never, ever feel deprived. To the contrary, when your everyday lifestyle is a healthy one, it doesn't really matter if you have that ice cream cone once in a while (sshhh ... don't tell Shani). You can really enjoy any food in its right time when you're conscious of overall balance.

It is my hope that no one will feel uncomfortable in their skin. And everyone should have healthy self-confidence and not let weight or cravings or preoccupation with food ever get in the way of so many more important things in life.

Best always,

Victoria

Hello from Shani

My clients have been begging me for this book since day one.

But I knew that I'd never do it until I could offer something complete and beautiful that people can use, whether dieting or just maintaining, including foods that don't feel like diet foods at all ... from simple meals for every day to dishes gourmet enough to serve at a *sheva berachos*.

I was brought up in a home of seven girls. And all of those girls were thin. Except me. As a child, I loved eating and was extremely overweight. When I was in 7th grade, I weighed between 160 and 170 pounds. My mother did not know what to do. It didn't matter that she put the right foods on the table. There was absolutely nothing she could do until I was personally ready. My oldest sister, who shared a room with me, would complain that she's too skinny, and I could never match my siblings. It wasn't fair. Why did I have this issue?

But I learned I could battle this issue.

When I was 13 years old, I decided I was ready to lose weight (and I tell all parents not to bring a child to me until that child is ready). I visited a nutritionist and subsequently lost all the excess weight.

But it was short-lived. When I was 14, I gained it back. All of it. All by eating fat-free foods.

So I tried again, this time visiting a different nutritionist. And I learned my lesson: endless fat-free foods weren't okay. But the right amount of a variety of foods, in moderation, certainly was. And I lost all that weight again, this time for good.

When I visited that first nutritionist, I told her that I ate three slices of pizza at a meal. She told me I can have pizza — but just one slice. I had to train myself to eat it slowly ... so that it would take the same amount of time to eat that one slice as it did to eat those three slices. It gave my brain time to process that I had actually eaten ... and that I was actually satisfied. Today, my clients are shocked that they can be so satisfied with less food.

When I made those changes, drinking water also became part of my lifestyle. Sometimes, thirst is mistaken for hunger, and I could squelch that craving by drinking two cups of water.

I believe that having that battle as a child helped make me a successful nutritionist today. I wouldn't understand my clients if I hadn't been there too. I do believe it's a battle every day, and I tell them that. Sometimes they'll say, "When are we done?"

I'll respond, "Are you ever done cleaning your house?"

If you neglect your home, it looks neglected.

Just as it needs maintenance every day, so does our healthy diet.

I believe in a well-balanced plan. Even vegetables are limited on my plan. All of my clients eat all food groups in moderation. A diet should be a way of life that you can live with forever. It doesn't mean not eating. It simply means that you know exactly what you're eating, even if it changes as time goes on, whether you want to lose weight or just maintain. In the beginning, I want my clients to use their calories for the most nutrient-dense and satisfying foods. But later on, a diet doesn't mean not eating a piece of cake. It means knowing that we ate that cake. Even sitting down to enjoy it with a fork.

A healthy person is never full and never hungry, just content and satisfied.

What do my clients do on Shabbos? Everyone has a customized plan so they can derive maximum enjoyment on that day and have the things they enjoy. Some have cholent, some don't. For bread, some enjoy matzah ... others have portioned challah rolls. Bake your 1- or 2-ounce challah rolls in muffin pans.

What's Inside

Recipes compatible with today's most common diets (Note: You may need to substitute some ingredients with diet compatible versions; e.g., gluten-free soy sauce for standard.)

Take note of serving sizes.

Calories for each recipe and the exchange on Shani's diet

A message from Victoria

Victoria's tips on making ahead, adapting the recipe for your entire family (who wants to cook twice?), and other serving ideas

Advice, info, and motivation from Shani

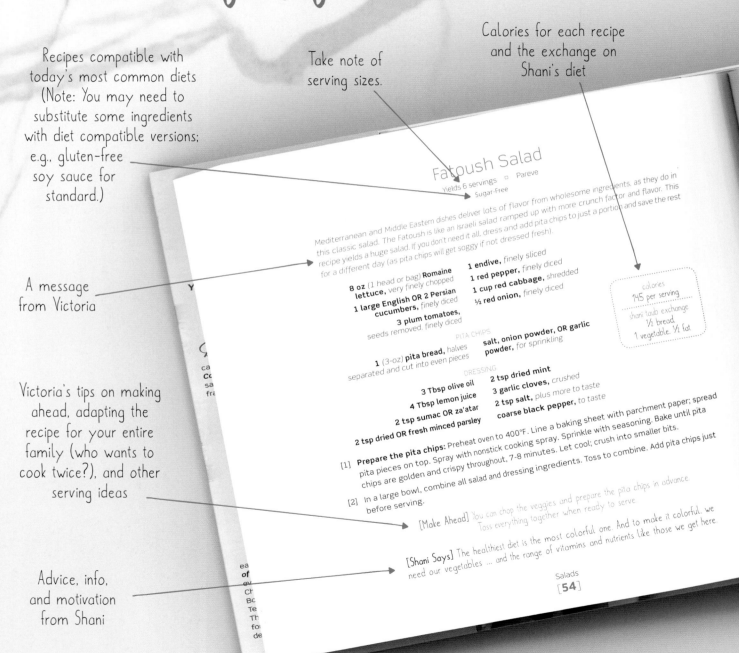

Fatoush Salad

Yields 6 servings □ Pareve
Sugar-Free

Mediterranean and Middle Eastern dishes deliver lots of flavor from wholesome ingredients, as they do in this classic salad. The Fatoush is like an Israeli salad ramped up with more crunch factor and flavor. This recipe yields a huge salad. If you don't need it all, dress and add pita chips to just a portion and save the rest for a different day (as pita chips will get soggy if not dressed fresh).

8 oz (1 head or bag) **Romaine lettuce,** very finely chopped
1 large **English OR 2 Persian cucumbers,** finely diced
3 **plum tomatoes,** seeds removed, finely diced

1 **endive,** finely sliced
1 **red pepper,** finely diced
1 cup **red cabbage,** shredded
½ **red onion,** finely diced

PITA CHIPS

1 (3-oz) **pita bread,** halves separated and cut into even pieces

salt, onion powder, OR garlic powder, for sprinkling

DRESSING

3 Tbsp olive oil
4 Tbsp lemon juice
2 tsp sumac OR za'atar
2 tsp dried OR fresh minced parsley

2 tsp dried mint
3 garlic cloves, crushed
2 tsp salt, plus more to taste
coarse black pepper, to taste

[1] **Prepare the pita chips:** Preheat oven to 400°F. Line a baking sheet with parchment paper; spread pita pieces on top. Spray with nonstick cooking spray. Sprinkle with seasoning. Bake until pita chips are golden and crispy throughout, 7-8 minutes. Let cool; crush into smaller bits.

[2] In a large bowl, combine all salad and dressing ingredients. Toss to combine. Add pita chips just before serving.

[Make Ahead] You can chop the veggies and prepare the pita chips in advance. Toss everything together when ready to serve.

[Shani Says] The healthiest diet is the most colorful one. And to make it colorful, we need our vegetables ... and the range of vitamins and nutrients like those we get here.

calories
145 per serving

shani taub exchange
½ bread,
1 vegetable, ½ fat

Salads
[54]

Do you use the MyFitnessPal app or website?

The calories for every recipe in **Secrets of Skinny Cooking** are preloaded on the app. There's no need to input every ingredient. Here's how to find these recipes:

1. Add "secretsofskinnycooking" as a friend.

2. Search through the public April and May 2017 Diary until you find the name of your desired recipe.

3. Click the three-dot icon to "Save as Meal."

You'll then have the recipe stored in your personal "Meals" to add quickly when logging your own entries.

Visit Victoria's kitchen and watch her prepare some of these dishes on Kosher.com's **Secrets of Skinny Cooking** show, available at kosher.com/shows/7/skinny-cooking.

How to Sauté and Caramelize Onions
Secrets
Without Oil

This is the method we use to sauté onions throughout this book.

→ Heat the pan over medium-high heat. You want your onions to sizzle when they hit that surface.

→ Lower heat and coat pan with nonstick cooking spray (for safety, you can turn off heat, spray, and turn it back on); add onions.

→ Sprinkle with salt. Salt draws the moisture out of the onions so they won't dry out!

→ Cover the pan! This will keep that moisture in.

→ Your onions will soften in 5-7 minutes, the same length of time as onions sautéed in oil. Then you can lift the lid, as there will be enough moisture in the pan. For golden, caramelized onions, simply keep cooking over low heat, stirring occasionally.

Caramelizing Onions with ... Sugar!

For truly delectable, caramelized sweet onions, you
can also caramelize with sugar! Add a teaspoon or two
of sugar to your onions in a greased sauté pan and cook on the
lowest heat, stirring occasionally. The sugar adds only 15 to 30
calories, compared to the 120 in a tablespoon of oil. It will take
time, but they will caramelize beautifully. These are worth it. You
can also season your caramelized onions with salt and pepper. Add
a bit of water to the pan to prevent them from burning before they
caramelize (the water will evaporate). We use these sweet golden
onions in the Caramelized Onion & Salmon Wraps (page 234).

Super-Light Caesar
(page 52)

Herb Balsamic
Vinaigrette
(page 174)

Basil-Lime Vinaigrette
(page 62)

Tahini-Style Dressing
(page 232)

Jars of Overnight Oats
in different flavors
(page 43)

45-Calorie Marinara
or Gourmet Chunky
Marinara
(page 156-157)

There are some things in life that, inevitably, take time. Having some common meal components ready and waiting for you in the fridge can make assembling meals super easy and super quick. Most of these items will stay fresh for a while. Here are some ideas of fridge staples you may want to keep on hand.

Secrets
Our Friend, the Fridge
(Didn't think we'd say that, right?)

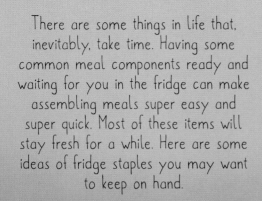

Cooked Quinoa

Miscellaneous Roasted Vegetables (eggplant, mushrooms, zucchini)

Pre-Cut Veggies (cucumbers, celery sticks, peppers, broccoli, tomatoes)

Sautéed Onions (page 16)

Roasted Peppers

Secrets
Yes, We Love Snacks

They're fun. They're the treats that keep you from rummaging through the freezer when you need that sweet or salty something after a meal. They're easy to grab when you're running out and won't have time for a meal till later. They give you something to look forward to when others are eating molten cake. Preparing meals might take a little time. Snacks, though, should be effortless. That's the point! Pictured are some of our store-bought favorites.

Some other ideas include:

→ Tea (Chai, Green, or your favorite) (0 calories)

→ Tofutti Chocolate Fudge Treats (30 calories)

→ Old-Fashioned Button Candy (40 calories)

→ Drizzilicious (90 Calories)

Manhattan Chocolates
Chocolate Leather
(50 calories)

↖ Matt's Munchies &
You Love Fruit Leather
(90 calories)

Sugar-Free
Gum

"Air"-Popped
Popcorn or
Store-Bought Light
Kettle Popcorn
(70 calories)

Hard Candy/Candy Drops
(such as Yum Earth,
14 calories)

Minute Maid
Juice Bars
(40 calories)

Brother's All Natural
Fruit Crisps
(45 calories)

Banana Soft-Serve
(page 31) ←

Strawberry Banana
Soft-Serve
(page 31)
↓

Breakfast

(at home or on the go)

Most days, you don't have time to open a cookbook to make breakfast. You need easy and filling concepts that can be pulled together in minutes or be made in advance ... like these. -Victoria

There's no way for a person to feel satiated throughout the day without breakfast. If you skip it, you'll end up snacking or eating a double lunch. You need much more food to fill you up when you're hungry. -Shani

Secrets
Dress Up Greek

Prefer your yogurt not-too-sweet? Add a packet of sweetener to plain yogurt in lieu of pre-sweetened varieties.

← The classic combo of fruit and granola is not overrated! Keep it seasonal and exciting ... pair your Greek with pomegranate and citrus in the winter, then peaches and blueberries in the summer. Top it with 2 tablespoons of our super low-cal Breakfast Granola (page 42).

← This one's super fun. Make your own Rice Krispies crunch by mixing 1 cup Rice Krispies with 1 teaspoon maple syrup. Spread on a baking sheet and bake at 350°F for 10 minutes. Sprinkle a couple of tablespoons on top of yogurt ... add some cinnamon, too.

Can't do without that cereal crunch in the morning? You don't have to! Add a few tablespoons of your favorite cereal to your yogurt and you'll be crunching throughout the creaminess ... for a fraction of the calories. →

↑
So you need chocolate and peanut butter? Add peanut butter powder (prepared according to package instructions) along with a half tablespoon of sugar-free mini chocolate chips (and maybe a tablespoon of Cocoa Krispies for extra crunch).

Yogurt doesn't need to be sweet to be satisfying. We also love plain Greek with savory ingredients such as fresh basil, a little lemon, chopped grape tomatoes, salt ... even diced cucumber. For another savory idea, try our Savory Warm Eggs & Yogurt (page 46).

Coffee in the cup; coffee in the bowl. Add some coffee, sweetener, and cinnamon to your yogurt. Or flavor it with sweetener and pure vanilla (or any flavor!) extract.

Add a natural burst of fruit flavor and crunch to your yogurt by adding whole or crushed pieces of freeze-dried fruit, such as Brother's Natural Fruit Crisps. We especially love the fruit powder at the bottom of the bag.

Yes, have your cake and yogurt too. When you don't want the calories of a whole muffin, take a quarter or half (depending on the size of that muffin) and crumble it into your Greek for muffin goodness in every bite.

Spread your toast with a bit of Greek yogurt or reduced-fat cream cheese and top with scrambled egg whites (or scrambled eggs with one yolk). ←

Pile the classic bruschetta topping over Melba toast (tomatoes, fresh basil, red onion, salt, pepper, and balsamic vinegar). ↑

Add crunch to your PB2 Toast with sliced celery, of course. ↖

Spread with a protein-packed spoon of chummus and top with Israeli salad. ←

Secrets
Put It on Toast
(or Rice Cakes)

Totally gourmet. Totally unexpected. Spread your toast with our Beet Pesto (page 78) and top with light feta (add herbs or microgreens if you like).

Victoria's all-time fav rice cake combo includes melted cheese + thinly sliced apple (sprinkle an ounce of finely shredded cheese on Pure Bites Pop Cakes for the most bang for your calorie buck).

Too good. Avocado (or our Avocado-Cucumber Cream, page 126), dried or fresh basil, & light feta or an egg-white omelette on top.

The Caprese
(page 30)

Secrets
Load That Frittata

Egg whites have the potential to be the perfect breakfast. They're low-calorie, high protein, and cook quickly. The problem? They need help in the flavor department, and they're not completely satisfying on their own. The good news is ... they're a blank slate and pair well with any cuisine. Here are our favorite ways to enjoy the simple egg.

→ Esti, our photographer, likes to add salsa to her omelette or frittata. It's easy, adds lots of flavor, and turns an omelette into a savory, hearty shakshuka-style meal with minimal calories. A little plain yogurt and fresh-squeezed lime make that omelette wow.

→ You can never go wrong with onions, especially if you keep a stock of oil-free sautéed onions in your fridge (see page 16). Simply add lots of onions to start and a little mozzarella to end and you can call that simple breakfast dish your French onion omelette.

→ Riff on our Eggplant Parmesan (page 160) by adding roasted eggplant, sauce, cauliflower cream, and a sprinkle of cheese ... so comforting!

→ Not all the additions have to happen while cooking. When I want to prepare eggs for a light meal that's later in the day (i.e., on a quiet Saturday night for Melave Malkah), I smear cooked egg whites with avocado and top with cabbage salad (like our Creamy Light Cole Slaw on page 78 or some simple red cabbage, as prepared on page 206) or, frankly ... whatever salad I have in the fridge! Enjoy with toast, matzah, or rice cakes.

→ And my absolute favorite egg white combo? The Caprese. So beautiful and satisfying. You'll find the recipe on page 30.

The Caprese

Yields 1 serving · Dairy
Gluten-Free · Low Carb · Sugar-Free

Though you can add almost anything to make your egg breakfast into a meal, this is the version I make most often, probably because I usually have these ingredients on hand. Keep sautéed onions in the fridge for quick prep in the morning. In my opinion, it's totally worthwhile to omit the yolks to be able to add cheese instead! And while you can make this in omelette or scrambled eggs format (and skip the oven), I love frittatas because of the way they puff up in the oven and seem much bigger than they are. If you're using a nonstick pan, it'll slide out perfectly onto your plate and look beautiful too.

½ **onion,** *diced*

¼ **tsp salt,** *plus more for sprinkling*

1 **Tbsp fresh minced basil leaves** *(or 3 frozen cubes)*

1 **tomato or ½ cup grape tomatoes,** *diced*

1 **cup fresh baby spinach leaves,** *optional*

3 **egg whites**

3 **Tbsp low-fat milk**

½ **oz shredded mozzarella cheese OR fresh mozzarella** *(even better!)*

calories
154 calories

shani taub exchange
1 protein

[1] Preheat oven to 400°F.

[2] Heat an oven-safe frying pan (if handle is plastic, cover in aluminum foil) over medium heat; coat very well with nonstick cooking spray. Lower heat, add onion (add basil cubes here if using instead of fresh leaves), and sprinkle with salt. Cover; cook until soft, 5-7 minutes, stirring occasionally.

[3] Raise heat; stir in basil, tomatoes, and spinach, if using. Cook an additional 1-2 minutes.

[4] In a cup, whisk together egg whites, milk, and ¼ teaspoon salt. Pour into pan (if you move the ingredients to either side and spray again, it will help the frittata release more easily). Top with cheese. Let cook for a few seconds, then transfer to oven. Bake for 10 minutes, until cheese is melted and egg appears set. Loosen edges with a spatula, slide onto a plate, and serve.

Banana Soft-Serve

Yields 1 serving ▫ Dairy
Gluten-Free ▫ Sugar-Free ▫ Low Carb

The next time you have extra-ripe bananas, don't bake banana bread. Peel and freeze them instead. Among all the yogurt mix-ins out there, I love my yogurt best with creamy, blended frozen bananas. Totally enjoy this ice cream for breakfast. The toppings make it even more fun.

1 *(5.3- or 6-oz)* **container plain or light vanilla Greek yogurt**

1 frozen banana, *chopped (may be chopped before or after freezing)*

TOPPINGS

1 Tbsp peanut butter powder *(such as PB2 or PBFit), mixed with 1 Tbsp water and 1 packet sweetener*

1 Tbsp Rice Krispies OR Rice Krispies Crunch *(page 24)*

calories
192 calories
(222 with toppings)

shani taub exchange
1 protein, 1 fruit
(toppings are extra)

[1] Add chopped frozen banana to a blender. Blend to combine. (It may look grainy but will become smooth when added to your bowl).

[2] In a bowl, stir together blended banana and yogurt. Add peanut butter mixture and Rice Krispies. Enjoy immediately.

[Try This!] Yes to variations! Try strawberry-banana soft-serve (using strawberry Greek yogurt) with puréed strawberries and granola (page 42) or Rice Krispies for crunch.

[Shani Says] Don't eat while standing! Sit down, use a spoon and fork, and enjoy every bite. The more slowly you eat, the more time the brain has to process that you actually ate and the more satisfied you'll be.

Protein Pancakes

Yields 12 pancakes   □   Dairy
Sugar-Free

I originally created this recipe to sneak protein into my picky kids, and they had no idea I secretly made their beloved pancakes healthy. Then I realized … with no sugar or fat and lots of added protein, these were a great guilt-free pancake option for grownups too … and I sat down and enjoyed the pancakes with them. Light vanilla yogurt will sweeten the pancakes without adding sugar (you can use plain yogurt if you prefer a pancake that's not sweet), and you can also try using white whole wheat flour if you like (add an additional tablespoon or so of milk).

1 cup flour
½ tsp baking soda
1 tsp baking powder
4 egg whites

1½ cups light vanilla or plain Greek yogurt
½ cup low-fat milk
1 tsp pure vanilla extract

calories
57 calories per pancake

shani taub exchange
3 pancakes =
1 bread, ¾ protein

[1]   In a medium bowl, combine flour, baking soda, and baking powder. Stir in egg whites, yogurt, milk, and vanilla.

[2]   Coat a skillet or pancake pan with nonstick cooking spray; heat over medium heat. Using a ¼-cup measuring cup, scoop up batter and add to pan. Cook until pancake bubbles and edges are set. Flip; cook on second side until golden.

[For the Family] Though my kids always insist on enjoying these pancakes with a syrup topping, I'm satisfied that they're happy with this healthier version. I'll even serve these as a kid-friendly breakfast-style dinner paired with a fruit shake (also secretly loaded with protein).

[Make Ahead] These freeze well! Make a double batch and keep some in a ziplock bag in the freezer. Microwave pancakes for a quick-prep morning meal.

[Shani Says] For a complete breakfast, enjoy 2 pancakes topped with a little more Greek yogurt or cottage cheese and fresh fruit.

French Toast Eggs-in-a-Hole

Yields 1 serving □ Dairy
Sugar-Free

One slice of toast? Eh, not so filling. A couple egg whites? Double eh, not filling at all. But ... put them together in a dish like this (and let cinnamon, vanilla, and sweetener help you out) ... now that's a great breakfast (and you can make the kid-friendly version at the same time!). And like breakfasts should, it takes just a couple of minutes to prep and cook. Tailor it to your own needs by adding more toast or egg whites (it's ok if they spill around the toast and don't all fit in the hole).

1 slice low-calorie whole wheat bread

2 egg whites

⅛ tsp cinnamon

½ tsp vanilla

2 Tbsp low-fat milk

2 packets Splenda or sweetener of choice

calories
113 calories

shani taub exchange
1 bread, ½ protein

[1] Using a small glass or cookie cutter, cut a circle from the center of the bread.

[2] In a shallow dish, whisk together egg whites, cinnamon, vanilla, milk, and sweetener. Dredge the bread slice and the cut-out circle in the mixture.

[3] Coat a frying pan with nonstick cooking spray. Heat over medium-high heat. Add bread and circle. Add remaining egg mixture to the center of the bread. Cook until bread is golden and egg is set on bottom; flip and cook on second side. Serve with a sprinkle of additional sweetener, if desired.

[For the Family] My kids love this dish. For them, I use whole eggs. Instead of sweetener in the batter, they enjoy this with maple syrup drizzled on top.

[Shani Says] Enjoy an iced coffee with ½ cup milk (or add 1 more egg white and use ⅓ cup milk) along with this breakfast for a complete, wholesome, and healthy meal with a complete serving of protein.

Apple Pie Crepes

Yields 10 crepes ▫ Dairy
Sugar-Free

It's really fun to stuff whatever you want inside a crepe. When I make a batch for my family for breakfast, I place a variety of fresh sliced fruit on the table. Once these are stuffed with yogurt and fruit, even just one crepe is super filling. But when crepes are low-cal like these, you can even have two.

CREPE BATTER

½ cup flour

1 egg

2 egg whites

½ cup milk

¾ cup light vanilla Greek yogurt

1 tsp almond or pure vanilla extract

pinch salt

FILLING (FOR 2 CREPES)

1 apple, *thinly sliced*

¼ tsp pure vanilla extract

1 tsp maple syrup

pinch cinnamon

6 Tbsp plain, light vanilla, OR favorite flavor light Greek yogurt OR cottage cheese

> **calories**
> 44 calories per crepe; 114 with apple filling
>
> **shani taub exchange**
> 2 fruit-filled crepes = 1 bread, 1 protein, 1 fruit

[1] In a blender, combine flour, egg, egg whites, milk, yogurt, extract, and salt. Blend to combine.

[2] Coat a crepe or frying pan well with nonstick cooking spray; heat over medium-high heat. Scoop ¼-cup batter into pan; swirl pan so batter covers bottom of pan. Cook until edges are brown and seem crispy. Slide a spatula under crepe and flip it. Cook for a few seconds on the second side and flip onto plate.

[3] Turn off heat; spray pan well again. Repeat with remaining batter.

[4] **Prepare the filling:** Coat a frying pan with nonstick cooking spray. Add apples and cook over medium-low heat until beginning to turn golden, about 4 minutes. Add vanilla, syrup, and cinnamon; cook for 1 more minute.

[5] To assemble, place 3 tablespoons yogurt or cottage cheese down the center of each crepe. Top with apples. Fold closed. Dust with additional sweetener, if desired.

[Make Ahead] Freeze crepes with a piece of parchment paper between them.

[Try This!] To make savory crepes, use plain Greek yogurt instead of vanilla, add a little salt to the batter, and stuff these with sautéed spinach and onions for a filling lunch.

Bagel Store Corn Muffins

Yields 10 muffins   ▫   Dairy

By the time I made my 25th batch, my kids had long since known to run away from me whenever I came at them holding corn muffins. I had given up. If I couldn't make a low-calorie corn muffin that tasted as good as the ones I buy at the bagel store, I was just not going to include it in this book. But I kept craving the muffins ... all I wanted in the morning was to grab one and go. Finally, on batch number 29 overall, I got it: a low-cal muffin we all wanted to finish straight out of the oven. Finally. Now, I can grab these for breakfast without wondering how many loads of calories are inside.

1 cup yellow cornmeal

¼ cup flour

½ cup granulated Splenda

2 tsp baking powder

¼ tsp baking soda

pinch salt

2 tsp pure vanilla extract

1 egg

1 cup light vanilla Greek yogurt

½ cup milk or soymilk

2 Tbsp oil

calories
105 calories per muffin

shani taub exchange
2 muffins =
1 bread, ½ protein, ⅓ fat

[1] Preheat oven to 400°F. Coat a 12-cup muffin pan very well with nonstick cooking spray.

[2] In a bowl, combine cornmeal, flour, Splenda, baking powder, baking soda, and salt. Add vanilla, egg, yogurt, milk, and oil. Stir until just combined.

[3] Divide batter among 10 muffin cups. Bake for 12-13 minutes, until muffins are firm on top and slightly golden at the edges.

[Good To Know] I prefer preparing these directly in a muffin pan without a cupcake liner so that the edges get all golden and crispy ... that's essential corn muffin criteria.

[Shani Says] An average bagel store corn muffin is about 4 ounces. These muffins are about 2¼ ounces each. With a 2-muffin serving size, you're getting more muffin (plus protein!) for just 210 calories!

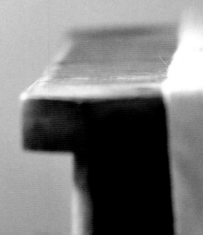

To make a coffee frappe,
add 1 cup each cooled coffee,
milk, and ice to a blender.
Add sweetener to taste.
Blend to combine.

Oat Bran Muffins

Yields 6 muffins □ Dairy
Sugar-Free

I'll admit, I don't understand how this recipe works! Shani forwarded this recipe to me, sharing that both she and her clients have been loving these muffins. But they didn't seem to make sense! Only 1 tablespoon of grains per muffin? Well, I might as well find out. I whisked together all the ingredients, filling 6 muffin cups all the way to the top (how did I get so much batter from so few ingredients?!?). Then, I watched how they rose beautifully, with results as fluffy as regular full-fat muffins. I still don't understand the science behind these muffins, but so what? Whether you call them oat bran muffins or magic muffins, enjoy 'em. Shani says you can eat three for breakfast.

6 Tbsp oat bran
1 Tbsp cinnamon
4 Tbsp granulated Splenda
1½ tsp baking powder
1 egg

2 egg whites
1 *(5.3-oz)* container light vanilla Greek yogurt
1 apple, *grated*
(optional, but recommended)

calories
58 calories per muffin

shani taub exchange
3 muffins =
1 bread, 1 protein

[1]   Preheat oven to 350°F. Line a muffin pan with 6 (or 7) cupcake liners.

[2]   In a bowl, combine oat bran, cinnamon, Splenda, and baking powder. Whisk in egg, egg whites, and yogurt. Fold in apple.

[3]   Divide batter among muffin cups; bake for 20 minutes, until tops are firm.

[Make Ahead] These will freeze beautifully. Keep a batch on hand always!

[Try This!] Don't like it when your muffin sticks to the cupcake liner? Use parchment liners instead and the entire muffin will release beautifully.

Breakfast Granola

Yields 5½ cups ▫ Pareve

The word "granola" has one of the healthiest connotations, and while healthy it may be, low-calorie it isn't. In traditional granola, oats are mixed with nuts, oil, and sugar, and baked until crisp … yielding a mixture that's super calorie-dense. But what if you want that crunch in your yogurt without the calories? Granola-lovers needed a solution! While this (fat-free) version is great as-is, feel free to use it as a base if you'd like to add your own selection of nuts and/or dried fruit. Add the nuts in Step 2 and the fruit after Step 3.

2½ cups quick cooking oats

2 cups each of 2 varieties of unsweetened breakfast cereal *(such as Rice Krispies, Corn Flakes, Rice Chex, Kashi cereals, Fiber One, Bran Flakes, Special K, or whole-grain varieties)*

1 Tbsp cinnamon

1 Tbsp vanilla

½ tsp salt

6 Tbsp maple syrup

2 egg whites

1 cup *(2 packets)* **Brother's All Natural Freeze-Dried Fruit Crisps** *(any flavor)*

calories
63 calories per
¼ cup serving

shani taub exchange
½ cup serving =
1 bread, 1 fruit

[1]   Preheat oven to 300°F. Line a baking sheet with parchment paper.

[2]   In a bowl, combine oats, cereals, cinnamon, vanilla, and salt. Stir in maple syrup and egg whites to coat.

[3]   Spread on prepared baking sheet; bake for 45 minutes, stirring every 15 minutes. Let cool. Add dried fruit. Store in an airtight container.

[Good to Know] Freeze-Dried Fruit Crisps have lots of fruity flavor with half the calories of dried fruit, but if you're adding dried fruit instead, choose unsweetened varieties. Dried apples, pears, peaches, and apricots are the least calorie-dense. Raisins and reduced-sugar Craisins come in next.

Lemon Poppy Overnight Oats

Yields 1 serving ▫ Dairy
Gluten-Free (use gluten-free oats) ▫ Sugar-Free

When I was in graduate school, to beat the traffic I used to leave my house in the morning while it was still dark outside. I'd stop at a local bagel store (the only place open at 5 a.m.) for my coffee and lemon poppy muffin, which I'd savor through my commute. I remember those muffins very, very well (but let's forget about the calories). I was still dreaming of that tart-and-sweet flavor one night this year, when, at 4 a.m. I couldn't fall back asleep. My brain was busy thinking of different overnight oat flavors inspired by my favorite muffins. I got up, prepped the oats in a few flavors, then went back to sleep. This one, of course, was my favorite.

1 *(5.3- or 6-oz)*
**container light
vanilla Greek yogurt**

**¼ cup quick cooking
or old-fashioned oats**

2 tsp lemon juice

1 tsp lemon zest,
plus more for garnish

1½ tsp poppy seeds

½ cup blueberries

calories
216 calories

shani taub exchange
1 protein, ¾ bread,
⅔ fruit

[1] **Do ahead:** In an 8-ounce jar or container, combine yogurt, oats, juice, zest, and poppy seeds. Add fruit and additional zest (on top or layered in the jar), either at this point or in the morning. Cover; leave overnight in the refrigerator.

[2] In the morning, open the jar and enjoy.

[Try This!] Keep different varieties of Overnight Oats (using various flavors of yogurt and fruit) in your fridge, ready to grab. They'll keep for at least a week. Don't add crunchy toppings until ready to enjoy. Having these ready will keep you from pouring that endless (yet convenient) bowl of cereal.

[Shani Says] Enjoy an even larger portion of these overnight oats for a fiber-loaded and filling one-bowl breakfast. Enjoy ⅓ cup raw oats and ¾ cups blueberries to get your complete protein, carb, and fruit (though you may need bigger jars).

How is it possible that these refreshing, indulgent,
and super-filling smoothies are so low in calories?
I love when we get a great bang for our buck!

Beets, Berries
(& Greens...
ssshh!)
↓

Strawberry
Cheesecake Smoothie
↓

Tropical
Cooler →

Tropical Cooler

Yields 1 large or 2 small smoothies　▫　Pareve
Gluten-Free

Canned crushed pineapple keeps it convenient, and you can certainly use thawed frozen mango instead of fresh.

½ **banana**

⅓ **cup canned crushed pineapple,** *in its own juice*

⅓ **cup very ripe diced mango**

3 **packets sweetener**

5 **ice cubes**

calories
135 calories
for entire recipe

shani taub exchange
1½ fruits

[1]　In a blender, combine all ingredients.

[2]　If you're using a small smoothie blender (that may not have room for all the ice), you can blend the other ingredients, then add ice and blend again.

Beets, Berries (& Greens ... ssshh!)

Yields 1 large shake　▫　Pareve
Gluten-Free　▫　Sugar-Free　▫　Low Carb

This smoothie tastes like an energizing health kick that's sweet and enjoyable too. If using fresh fruit instead of frozen, use ⅓ less liquid.

1 **large beet,** *cooked and peeled (vacuum-sealed beets work well)*

1 **cup no- or low-calorie fruit juice** *(we used Bai 5)*

6 **frozen strawberries OR ⅓ cup frozen blueberries**

½ **cup kale OR baby spinach leaves** *(optional)*

calories
83 calories
for entire recipe

shani taub exchange
1 fruit

▫　Blend all ingredients until smooth.

Strawberry Cheesecake Smoothie

Yields 2 medium smoothies　▫　Dairy
Gluten-Free　▫　Sugar-Free　▫　Low Carb

6 **frozen strawberries**

1 *(5.3-oz)* **container light vanilla Greek yogurt**

1 **cup low-fat milk**

1 **Tbsp sugar-free vanilla pudding powder**

½ **cup ice**

calories
119 calories
per serving

shani taub exchange
1 protein, ½ fruit
per serving

[1]　In a blender, combine strawberries, yogurt, milk, pudding powder, and ice. Blend until smooth.

[2]　If you're using a small smoothie blender (that may not have room for all the ice), you can blend the other ingredients, then add ice and blend again.

Savory Warm Eggs & Yogurt

Yields 1 serving   □   Dairy
Gluten-Free   □   Low Carb (without toast)   □   Sugar-Free

Whenever I want an all-protein breakfast, I combine yogurt and egg whites into one dish ... and I always add savory flavors instead of sweet. The combination of hot and cold components also makes this refreshing and comforting at the same time. It's so different from the usual fruit-and-yogurt parfait. Feel free to adjust the quantities of yogurt or egg whites to your liking. You can also make this crepe-style and stuff the yogurt into the egg white omelette (you'll need more egg whites).

½ cup plain Greek yogurt
sea salt, *for sprinkling*
dried basil, *for sprinkling*
garlic powder, *for sprinkling*
3 egg whites

2 tsp fresh minced basil
(or 2 frozen cubes)
pinch salt
1 slice whole wheat toast,
optional

calories
117 calories
(excluding toast)

shani taub exchange
1 protein;
add 1 bread per
slice of toast

[1] Spread Greek yogurt onto your plate; sprinkle with sea salt, dried basil, and garlic powder.

[2] Coat a frying pan with nonstick cooking spray; heat over medium heat. Whisk together egg whites, fresh basil, and salt (if using frozen basil cubes, add them to the pan first over low heat to defrost). Add egg white mixture to pan; cook until eggs are set, flipping midway.

[3] Top yogurt with omelet; sprinkle with additional dried basil and sea salt. Enjoy alongside a slice of whole wheat toast, if desired.

[Shani Says] Life becomes more exciting with a little seasoning!
Diets don't have to be boring — they can be fun!

I always tell my clients … "Don't eat the salads at a simchah. Those are loaded with oil, mayo, and sugar. Eat your salad at home." Their own salads, which they prep themselves, will be healthier and more filling. Then they can eat the main dish at the simchah and feel great. -Shani

The official ratio of oil to vinegar in a French vinaigrette is 3:1! I don't care what's official. Flavor can come from lots of places and a salad does not need to be covered in oil to taste good. -Victoria

Salads

(on the side or as a main)

Secrets
How to Make Low-Cal Dressings Using Whatever's in the Pantry

Creamy Without Calories

→ Start with light (35 calories per tablespoon), low-fat (15 calories per tablespoon), or canola-based (40 calories per tablespoon, for those concerned about cholesterol) mayonnaise. Mayonnaise doesn't have the best reputation, but it deserves better! Dressings based on lower-fat versions of mayo give you so much more quantity for the calories.

→ Add a little bit of acid (vinegar or lemon/lime juice) for flavor. Add water! Mayo does need to be thinned to desired consistency.

→ Whisk in all your herbs and seasonings. With lots of fresh herbs, fresh garlic or minced shallots, dried spices, mustards ... there are plenty of no-cal and low-cal flavor options.

Whisk Your Vinaigrette

→ Start by adding your vinegar to a bowl. Though you can use white vinegar, other options such as apple cider, rice, or wine vinegars give you additional calorie-free flavor. Add other acids, such as lemon or lime juice, now too (or instead of vinegar). Balsamic vinegar is very strong when not balanced with lots of olive oil. You can swap half your balsamic for red wine vinegar for more balanced flavor.

→ Bulk it up with herbs and seasoning. Fresh garlic, fresh basil, dried spices, salt, and pepper can all be whisked in now.

→ Add an emulsifier. A pinch of mustard or low-fat mayo keeps the vinegar and oil from separating.

→ If you want a sweet dressing, you can also whisk in your sweetener, or a tablespoon of honey, maple syrup, jam, or silan (the latter options will all add calories, so use sparingly).

→ Water! In the absence of lots of oil, you do need some water to calm the strong vinegar taste. A tablespoon or two will do.

→ Lastly, whisk in your olive oil. You do need a little, but at this point you can get away with just 1 tablespoon and still have great vinaigrette!

Super Light Caesar

Yields 4 servings □ Dairy
Gluten-Free (without croutons) □ Low Carb (without croutons) □ Sugar-Free

That Caesar salad you ordered at a restaurant because you wanted something light? It can likely contain about 1,000 calories. Caesar dressing is usually made with full-fat mayo, or, traditionally, an emulsion of egg yolks and olive oil, and contains about 100 calories per tablespoon. Compare that to this version, which only has 14 (and will be finished down to the last lettuce leaf, just the same)! When low-fat mayonnaise is used instead of light, the dressing is virtually calorie-free.

SALAD

12 oz *(1½ heads or bags)*
chopped Romaine lettuce

3 Tbsp Parmesan cheese

3 Tbsp croutons *(optional)*

LIGHT CAESAR DRESSING

¼ cup light mayonnaise

2 Tbsp water

2 Tbsp lemon juice

2 Tbsp white wine vinegar

1 garlic clove, *crushed*

½ tsp Dijon mustard

¼ tsp Worcestershire sauce

½ tsp salt

pinch coarse black pepper

calories
79 calories per serving
(with croutons)

shani taub exchange
1 fat, ¼ protein

[1] **Prepare the dressing:** In a bowl, whisk together mayonnaise, water, lemon juice, vinegar, garlic, mustard, Worcestershire sauce, salt, and pepper until smooth.

[2] Toss lettuce with dressing, croutons (if using), and Parmesan; serve.

[Make Ahead] Caesar dressing always comes in handy. Make a big batch and keep it in your fridge for always.

[Shani Says] Make your salad more filling and satisfying by making your croutons from whole wheat 100-calorie rolls, such as those made by Stern's or Franczoz (add 1 bread to your meal), as shown on page 58.

Fatoush Salad

Yields 6 servings ▫ Pareve

Sugar-Free

Mediterranean and Middle Eastern dishes deliver lots of flavor from wholesome ingredients, as they do in this classic salad. The Fatoush is like an Israeli salad ramped up with more crunch factor and flavor. This recipe yields a huge salad. If you don't need it all, dress and add pita chips to just a portion and save the rest for a different day (as pita chips will get soggy if not dressed fresh).

8 oz *(1 head or bag)* **Romaine lettuce,** *very finely chopped*

1 large English OR 2 Persian cucumbers, *finely diced*

3 plum tomatoes, *seeds removed, finely diced*

1 endive, *finely sliced*

1 red pepper, *finely diced*

1 cup red cabbage, *shredded*

½ red onion, *finely diced*

PITA CHIPS

1 *(3-oz)* **pita bread,** *halves separated and cut into even pieces*

salt, onion powder, OR garlic powder, *for sprinkling*

DRESSING

3 Tbsp olive oil

4 Tbsp lemon juice

2 tsp sumac OR za'atar

2 tsp dried OR fresh minced parsley

2 tsp dried mint

3 garlic cloves, *crushed*

2 tsp salt, *plus more to taste*

coarse black pepper, *to taste*

calories
145 calories per serving

shani taub exchange
½ bread,
1 vegetable, ½ fat

[1] **Prepare the pita chips:** Preheat oven to 400°F. Line a baking sheet with parchment paper; spread pita pieces on top. Spray with nonstick cooking spray. Sprinkle with seasoning. Bake until pita chips are golden and crispy throughout, 7-8 minutes. Let cool; crush into smaller bits.

[2] In a large bowl, combine all salad and dressing ingredients. Toss to combine. Add pita chips just before serving.

[Make Ahead] You can chop the veggies and prepare the pita chips in advance. Toss everything together when ready to serve.

[Shani Says] The healthiest diet is the most colorful one. And to make it colorful, we need our vegetables ... and the range of vitamins and nutrients like those we get here.

Italian Roasted Cauliflower Salad

Yields 4 servings ◻ Dairy
Gluten-Free ◻ Low Carb ◻ Sugar-Free

I'm so appreciative to those in the kosher industry who constantly work to bring a bigger range of kosher insect-free produce to store shelves …. including fresh cauliflower. Though I use versatile frozen cauliflower throughout this book, this salad needs the crispness of fresh.

12 oz fresh cauliflower florets
½ tsp dried basil
½ tsp dried oregano
½ tsp garlic powder
½ tsp salt

8 oz *(1 head or bag)* **chopped Romaine lettuce**
1 cup grape tomatoes, *halved*
½ bell pepper, *diced*
1½ oz light feta cheese, *crumbled*
1 Tbsp capers

HERB VINAIGRETTE

2 Tbsp white wine vinegar
1 Tbsp water
1 Tbsp fresh minced basil
(or 3 frozen cubes)
1 Tbsp fresh minced parsley
(or 3 frozen cubes)

½ tsp dried oregano
½ tsp salt
pinch coarse black pepper
1 garlic clove, *crushed*
½ tsp Dijon mustard
1 Tbsp olive oil

calories
87 calories per serving

shani taub exchange
1 vegetable,
1 protein, 1 fat
for entire recipe

[1] Preheat oven to 450°F. Line a baking sheet with parchment paper; coat with nonstick cooking spray.

[2] Spread cauliflower florets on baking sheet; sprinkle with basil, oregano, garlic powder, and salt. Spray with nonstick cooking spray. Bake for 20 minutes.

[3] In a large bowl, toss together lettuce, cauliflower, tomatoes, pepper, feta cheese, and capers.

[4] **Prepare the dressing:** In a small bowl, whisk together all vinaigrette ingredients.

[5] Toss salad with dressing before serving.

[Good To Know] I use capers here for that briny, Italian-inspired flavor without the calories of olives. I'll dress up this salad for company by adding some gourmet olives.

[Shani Says] Why share? Enjoy the entire salad as a meal.

Creamy Kale Salad

Yields 4 servings □ Dairy
Gluten-Free □ Low Carb

Light and low-fat varieties of mayonnaise are really great when it comes to giving you lots of dressing for the calories (and we love them for that), but they don't contribute much nutritionally. Ah, but when mayo can't step up, Greek yogurt can. This is feel-good all around.

1 lb butternut squash, *cubed*

salt, *for sprinkling*

5 oz kale

1 slice low-calorie whole wheat bread, *cut into cubes* **OR**
3 Tbsp croutons *(optional)*

½ tsp garlic powder *(optional)*

CREAMY HERB DRESSING

1 *(6-oz)* **container plain nonfat Greek yogurt**

2 Tbsp lemon juice

1 tsp Worcestershire sauce

1 tsp Dijon mustard

2 garlic cloves, *crushed*

½ cup fresh basil leaves OR
2 Tbsp fresh minced basil
(or 6 frozen cubes)

½ tsp salt

4 grinds fresh ground black pepper

1 Tbsp olive oil

> calories
> 115 calories per serving
> without bread
>
> shani taub exchange
> 1 bread,
> ¼ protein, ¼ fat
> per serving

[1] Preheat oven to 450°F. Line a baking sheet with foil; coat with nonstick cooking spray.

[2] Spread butternut squash on baking sheet, sprinkle with salt, and coat with nonstick cooking spray. Bake for 50 minutes.

[3] **Prepare the optional croutons:** Place bread cubes into a small baking pan. Coat with nonstick cooking spray; sprinkle with salt and garlic powder. Add to oven; bake until crisp, 5-7 minutes, shaking pan midway through.

[4] **Prepare the dressing:** Whisk together dressing ingredients.

[5] In a large bowl, toss kale and squash with ⅔-¾ cup dressing (you will have extra dressing). Let sit for a few minutes to allow the dressing to soften the kale before serving.

> [Shani Says] Kale is one of the healthiest lettuce greens around ... the deep green means it's full of fiber and it's super low in calories. In reference to all lettuces, I tell my clients, "Just go and enjoy. You don't need to count." Butternut squash, though, is a high-carb veggie, so I count 8 ounces of it as 1 bread.

Forever Crunchy Snap Pea Salad

Yields 6 servings ▫ Pareve
Gluten-Free ▫ Low Carb ▫ Sugar-Free

I didn't know that my friend was both gluten- and lactose-intolerant when I invited her over for a dairy meal. While everyone else was eating pizza, pasta, arancini balls, and homemade ice cream, there was absolutely nothing that she could have ... except this salad (all the other salads were dairy, of course). I had thrown it together earlier that afternoon. It's a good thing she enjoyed it ... and it's a good thing she asked for the recipe right away, so I'd have a text message account of what I actually did.

12 oz sugar snap peas, *halved*

1 red pepper, *very thinly sliced (preferably on a mandoline)*

10 oz shredded red cabbage

3 carrots, *peeled and julienned*

6-8 radishes, *cut into matchsticks*

DRESSING

¼ cup soy sauce

¼ cup rice vinegar

¼ cup water

1 Tbsp sesame oil

3 packets sweetener

1 Tbsp fresh minced ginger

2 garlic cloves, *crushed*

pinch coarse black pepper

> calories
> 82 calories per serving
>
> shani taub exchange
> ⅙ vegetable, ⅓ fat
> per serving

[1] In a large bowl, combine sugar snap peas, red pepper, red cabbage, carrots, and radishes.

[2] **Prepare the dressing:** In a jar or cruet, combine soy sauce, rice vinegar, water, sesame oil, sweetener, ginger, garlic, and black pepper.

[3] Toss with salad. This salad is best if dressed a little while before serving so the flavors have time to meld.

Arugula-Mango Salad
with Basil-Lime Vinaigrette

Yields 4 servings □ Pareve
Gluten-Free □ Low Carb □ Sugar-Free

When I visit my mother, I usually assemble an impromptu salad for lunch. That entails looking through the produce drawers and figuring out something that works using items I have available. When all I can find are the basics — like cucumbers and tomatoes — I often prefer to go with fruit ... and enjoy something like this. And no, it's not a mistake; there is no oil in this dressing. You're welcome to add a tablespoon if you like, but with bitter, sweet, and sour flavors working together (Arugula + Fruit + Lime = Great Combo!), you won't miss it.

4 oz arugula   **1 apple**
1 ripe mango, *sliced*   **1 Tbsp sunflower seeds**
1 peach OR nectarine, *sliced*

BASIL-LIME VINAIGRETTE
2 Tbsp apple cider vinegar   **½ tsp garlic powder**
2 Tbsp lime juice *(from about 1 lime)*   **½ tsp salt**
2 Tbsp water   **2 packets sweetener**
2 Tbsp fresh minced basil
(or 6 frozen cubes)

calories
101 calories per serving

shani taub exchange
1 fruit

[1] In a large bowl, toss together arugula, mango, and peach.

[2] **Prepare the dressing:** In a bowl, whisk together vinegar, lime juice, water, basil, garlic powder, salt, and sweetener.

[3] Peel and dice apple; toss in vinaigrette.

[4] Add vinaigrette and apples to salad. Top with sunflower seeds; toss to combine.

[Good To Know] Crisp, diced apples are a great stand-in for crunchy croutons. Just add an acid to prevent browning.

[Try This!] You can use 2 mangoes when stone fruit is not in season.

The Red Salad

Yields 4 servings □ Pareve
Gluten-Free □ Low Carb □ Sugar-Free □ Whole30 □ Paleo

This refreshing dish (and all its seasonal fruit) is one of the things I love about winter. And though it used to take a commitment of time to prepare, now that I've figured out a "cheating" way of supreming oranges, it no longer does. To "supreme" an orange with less work and less waste, first peel the orange with a knife, exposing the fruit. Then, simply slice the fruit vertically through the middle of each segment. Don't separate into segments by hand or the not-as-pretty-or-tasty pith will be exposed.

4 large beets	**½ red onion,** *finely diced*
3 oranges, *supremed*	**juice of 1-2 limes**
1 red grapefruit, *supremed*	**1 Tbsp olive oil**
seeds of 1 pomegranate	**salt,** *to taste*

calories
182 calories per serving

shani taub exchange
2 fruits, ¼ fat

[1] Preheat oven to 425°F. Wash beets; wrap each in foil. Place wrapped beets directly into oven (or use a baking pan) and bake until soft, about 1 hour. Let cool, rub off peel, and slice into wedges.

[2] In a bowl, combine beets, oranges, grapefruit, pomegranate seeds, and red onion. It's ok if the color of the beets bleeds into the salad after you toss it; after all, this is a red salad. Dress with lime juice, olive oil, and salt to taste.

[Shani Says] Beets are one of the highest fiber vegetables, but because of their sugar content, I count 2 beets as 1 fruit.

Friday Rice Salad

Yields 2 servings □ Pareve
Gluten-Free □ Low Carb

When I was a teenager, whenever my mother would make something calorie-dense, such as baked ziti, for dinner, I'd first take a bag of lettuce from the refrigerator. I'd empty half the lettuce into my bowl, then add some ziti and a little light dressing. By turning a portion of ziti into a "ziti salad," I could "stretch" a smaller portion of ziti into a larger, more filling meal. Today, I sometimes do the same thing on Fridays when I'm hungry for lunch and there's a fresh pot of white rice that I just prepared for Shabbat on the stove. I can either enjoy a cup of rice … and perhaps not be so satisfied … or I can make a big rice salad (that takes much longer to eat) and be very satisfied for less than half the calories.

8 oz *(1 head or bag)* **chopped Romaine lettuce**

1 cup shredded cabbage or coleslaw mix

½ cup cooked white rice

½ cucumber, *peeled and diced*

1 apple, *diced* **OR ¼ cup croutons**

calories
164 calories per serving

shani taub exchange
½ bread, ½ fruit, 1 fat
per serving

SWEET GARLIC DRESSING

2 Tbsp light mayonnaise

2 Tbsp water

1 Tbsp vinegar

2 garlic cloves, *crushed*

1 tsp salt

2 packets sweetener

[1] In a bowl, toss together lettuce, cabbage, rice, cucumber, and apple (for crunch).

[2] **Prepare the dressing:** In a small bowl, whisk together mayonnaise, water, vinegar, garlic, salt, and sweetener.

[3] Toss with salad before serving.

[Shani Says] This is the best way to stretch a grain … add veggies!

Greek-Style Quinoa

Yields 4 servings   □   Dairy

One of the benefits of preparing lots of dishes for each photo shoot was that I'd have plenty of food prepped and ready in the fridge to enjoy for the rest of the week. It didn't matter if I got way too busy to prep lunch for myself. Lunch was already done! During that time, one of my favorite go-to lunch dishes became this quinoa salad. It's super filling and the crunchy veggies stay crisp all week long. Make it ahead, no prob.

1¼ cups cooked quinoa

1 yellow pepper, *diced*

1 orange pepper, *diced*

1½ cups grape tomatoes, *halved*

1 red onion, *finely diced*

1 English cucumber,
sliced into ribbons

DRESSING

5 Tbsp red wine vinegar

2 Tbsp water

1 tsp Dijon mustard

1 tsp dried basil

1 tsp dried oregano

1 tsp garlic powder

1 tsp salt

pinch coarse black pepper

1 Tbsp olive oil

calories
186 calories per serving

shani taub exchange
¾ bread,
1 vegetable, ¼ fat
per serving

TOPPING

3-5 olives per serving

1½ oz feta cheese, *shredded*

[1] In a large bowl, combine quinoa, peppers, tomatoes, onion, and cucumber ribbons.

[2] **Prepare the dressing:** In a small bowl or jar, whisk together vinegar, water, mustard, basil, oregano, garlic powder, salt, and pepper. Whisk in olive oil.

[3] Toss dressing with salad. Top with feta and olives.

New Roasted Nicoise Salad

Yields 2 servings ▫ Pareve

Gluten-Free ▫ Low Carb ▫ Sugar-Free ▫ Whole30 and Paleo (both with alternative mustard)

Although tuna (which I love) is typically used in a Nicoise salad, I like salmon here. That's because I can roast the salmon and green beans on one baking sheet (no pots!), then simply toss with the other ingredients and dressing. Salmon shreds easily, so you can get a little of everything in each bite. Canned tuna would also work in this one-dish meal.

¾ lb. skinless salmon fillet *(or tuna steak, see note)*

1 lb French green beans

5 tsp salt, *plus more for sprinkling*

coarse black pepper, *for sprinkling*

2 Tbsp PLUS 1 tsp Dijon mustard, *divided*

4 Tbsp lemon juice, *divided*

1 cup tomatoes, *sliced*

1 small pickle, *diced, optional*

2 hard-boiled eggs, *optional*

2 Tbsp white wine vinegar

3 garlic cloves, *crushed*

¼ cup fresh chopped parsley leaves

¼ red onion, *finely diced*

calories
305 calories per serving (without egg)

shani taub exchange
2 proteins, ¾ vegetable per serving (without egg)

[1] Preheat oven to 400°F. Line a baking sheet with parchment paper; coat with nonstick cooking spray. Place salmon fillet (see note for preparing this dish with fresh tuna) and green beans on baking sheet. Sprinkle with salt and pepper. Whisk together 2 tablespoons mustard and 2 tablespoons lemon juice; spread over salmon. Bake for 20 minutes, or until salmon flakes easily with a fork.

[2] In a container, combine green beans, tomatoes, pickle (if using), white wine vinegar, remaining 2 tablespoons lemon juice, remaining 1 teaspoon mustard, garlic, parsley, red onion, and salt. Cover and shake to combine. Serve alongside salmon and eggs, if desired. Shred fish and toss with salad when ready to enjoy.

[Try This!] To prepare this dish with tuna, as shown, simply season tuna with salt and pepper and sear over medium-high heat in a skillet coated with nonstick cooking spray for about 1 minute per side. Slice thinly and toss with green beans.

Thai Chicken Salad

Yields 2 servings ◻ Meat

Gluten-Free ◻ Low Carb ◻ Sugar-Free ◻ Whole30 ◻ Paleo

One pan, fifteen minutes, and this beautiful complete dinner is on the table.

2 red onions, *thinly sliced*

¾ lb skinless, boneless chicken breasts, *thinly sliced*

2 garlic cloves, *crushed*

salt, *for sprinkling*

coarse black pepper, *for sprinkling*

SALAD

3 cups shredded cabbage OR Napa Cabbage, *thinly sliced*

4 carrots, *julienned*

1 red pepper, *diced*

½ cup fresh basil leaves, *chopped*

½ cup chopped scallions, *for garnish*

sesame seeds, *for garnish*

calories
349 calories per serving

shani taub exchange
2 proteins,
1 vegetable, ⅓ fat

DRESSING

3 Tbsp rice vinegar

3 Tbsp lime juice

2 tsp sesame oil

1 Tbsp minced fresh ginger *(or 3 frozen cubes)*

1 garlic clove, *crushed*

1 packet sweetener

[1] Heat a sauté pan over high heat. Lower heat, coat with nonstick cooking spray, and add onions. Cover; cook for 5 minutes.

[2] Season chicken with garlic, salt, and pepper. Uncover pan; push onions to the side. Spray pan with additional cooking spray; add chicken to pan and cook, 3-4 minutes per side. Remove from pan and slice into strips. If any slices are still raw in the center, return them to the pan and continue to sauté until done.

[3] **Prepare the dressing:** Whisk together dressing ingredients.

[4] In a bowl, combine cabbage, carrots, pepper, basil, and chicken/onion mixture. Toss with dressing. Top with scallions and sesame seeds.

[Try This!] Add some extra crunch! For 50 additional calories per serving, add 2 tablespoons peanuts or cashews to this salad. I also like it with crispy wonton strips for 40 extra calories per serving: Slice 4 wonton wrappers into thin strips, spray with nonstick cooking spray, season with salt and garlic, and bake at 400°F until crisp, about 4 minutes.

Chickpea Salad with Honey-Lemon Vinaigrette

Yields 4 servings □ Meat
Gluten-Free □ Low Carb

My mother-in-law told me she had enjoyed the most delicious chicken salad from the takeout department of Seasons in Lakewood. The next time I was there, I visited the takeout counter. No salads.

"Do you know if you have a chicken salad with chickpeas?" I asked the man behind the counter. He didn't.

Later, while I was in the produce department, he ran up to me. "Now I remember! There was a salad our chef had put together as a one-time thing at the spur of the moment."

I got more details. Kale, not Romaine. Mushrooms, cooked. Peppers, fresh. A honey-lemon vinaigrette. Then I went home and made this.

8 oz baby bella mushrooms, *sliced*

2 Tbsp water

5 oz kale

1 red pepper, *diced*

¾ cup canned or cooked chickpeas

6 oz fresh broccoli
(omit if fresh is unavailable)

8 oz oven-roasted turkey breast, *diced* **OR 2 grilled chicken breasts,** *sliced into strips*

HONEY-LEMON VINAIGRETTE

3 Tbsp lemon juice

2 Tbsp vinegar

1 Tbsp honey

3 packets sweetener

1½ tsp salt

pinch coarse black pepper

3 garlic cloves, *crushed*

1 Tbsp oil

> calories
> 175 calories per serving
>
> shani taub exchange
> ½ salad =
> 2 proteins, 1 vegetable,
> ⅓ fat

[1] Coat a sauté pan with nonstick cooking spray; heat over high heat. Add mushrooms (you should hear a sizzle when the mushrooms hit the pan). Add 2 tablespoons water; sauté, about 3-4 minutes, until mushrooms are browned.

[2] In a large bowl, combine kale, red pepper, chickpeas, and broccoli, if using.

[3] **Prepare the vinaigrette:** In a small bowl, whisk together vinaigrette ingredients.

[4] Add dressing to salad. Using a gloved hand, massage vinaigrette into kale. Add mushrooms and turkey; toss well to coat, scooping up vinaigrette from the bottom of the bowl.

↑
Pink Pickles
(page 79)

Shabbos Salads & Dips

Remake your Shabbos table with lots of fun and flavorful dips, salads, and spreads that are a tiny fraction of the calories of the usual mayo-based options. You can find these dips on the following page and throughout this book.

↖ Avocado-
Cucumber Cream
(page 126)

Creamy Light
Cole Slaw
(page 78)

Eggplant Puree
(page 130)

Beet Pesto,
(page 78)

Turkish Salad
(page 80)

Beet Pesto

Yields 1 cup ▢ Pareve
Gluten-Free ▢ Low Carb ▢ Sugar-Free ▢ Whole30 ▢ Paleo

I can eat this spread on its own by the spoonful. Though you can't see the nuts (unlike in a traditional pesto), you can taste them, so don't leave them out!

2 large or 3 medium ready-cooked vacuum-sealed beets
1 Tbsp olive oil
1 Tbsp water

1 large or 2 small garlic cloves
1 Tbsp pine nuts OR chopped nuts
½ tsp salt

calories
15 calories
per tablespoon

shani taub exchange
Free

[1] In a blender, combine beets, olive oil, water, garlic, nuts, and salt. Blend until smooth.

[2] Enjoy pesto as a dip, or spread onto toast.

[Shani Says] Enjoy 1 tablespoon of beet pesto free as a dip or spread.

Creamy Light Cole Slaw

Yields 5 cups ▢ Pareve
Gluten-Free ▢ Low Carb ▢ Sugar-Free

While working on Everyday Secret Restaurant Recipes, *I visited the kitchen of the takeout department where my favorite coleslaw is made. That version, I thought, tastes so fresh and healthy ... it must be lighter than other store-bought versions. Wrong. Hidden throughout that freshly shredded cabbage was loads of full-fat mayo and sugar. I still love that slaw, but I also enjoy this one without second-guessing every bite.*

5 cups *(11 oz)* **shredded cabbage or coleslaw mix**
1-2 carrots, *shredded*
(omit if using coleslaw mix)
¼ cup light mayonnaise

½ tsp salt
dash black pepper
dash celery seed
1½ Tbsp white wine vinegar
4 packets sweetener

calories
50 calories per cup

shani taub exchange
1¼ cups = 1 fat

[1] Place half the cabbage into a bowl. Add carrots, mayonnaise, salt, pepper, celery seed, and vinegar.

[2] Stir in remaining cabbage, 1 cup at a time. Stir in sweetener, 1 packet at a time, as you add the cabbage. Slaw can be made up to 2 days in advance and stored in the fridge.

Pink Pickles

Yields 2 (1-quart) Mason jars ▫ Pareve
Gluten-Free ▫ Low Carb ▫ Whole30 and Paleo (omit sugar)

This is a staple on my Shabbat table. I make a big batch at a time, fill-ing a few Mason jars. They last for several weeks until I use them all up. Pink pickles are crunchy, satisfying, and refreshing, and a great mostly calorie-free item to nibble on instead of more challah during that first course (or at the end of the meal when you're simply shmoozing around the table ... another challah-eating time). It's ok if you have only turnips or cauliflower and not both, but you need the beets to turn everything pink! I included these pickles in tiny Mason jars in my mishloach manot last year.

2 lb sliced turnips AND/OR fresh cauliflower

1 beet, *peeled and sliced*

3 garlic cloves

1½ cups apple cider vinegar

2¼ cups water

1½ Tbsp pickling spice

5 Tbsp salt

1½ Tbsp sugar

calories
19 calories
for ½ cup pickles

shani taub exchange
Free

[1]   Pack 2 (1-quart) Mason jars with turnips; top with beet slices. Add garlic.

[2]   In a saucepan, combine vinegar, water, pickling spice, salt, and sugar. Bring to a simmer to dissolve salt and sugar.

[3]   Pour liquid into jars over vegetables. Make sure the liquid comes all the way to the top. Seal tightly. Leave jars on the counter in a sunny place for 12 hours, then refrigerate for 12 hours before serving. Pickles will last indefinitely in the refrigerator.

[Shani Says] Yes, this is also free! It's salty, but because it's a vegetable, and you're likely only having a few slices, you can munch without counting.

Turkish Salad

Yields 3 cups ▫ Pareve

Gluten-Free ▫ Low Carb ▫ Sugar-Free ▫ Whole30 and Paleo (without sweetener)

Shabbos salads, dips, and salatim are such a personal thing … every community and culture has its own. What I also learned, when I started exploring the salatim of other people's Shabbat tables so I can give you some light options, is that everyone makes them differently! Turkish Salad, it seemed, had no consistent definition. I knew I wanted a sweet and spicy tomato-based type of salad. Some versions had eggplant (and you can certainly add roasted eggplant). Some versions were cooked … but I was intrigued by this no-cook technique of simply combining all the ingredients and that's it! The flavor is so bright and fresh, and this makes a really big quantity, enough for several weeks, so the olive oil really becomes negligible. This time you can really dip and dip … and dip!

1 red pepper, *cut into large chunks*

1 green pepper, *cut into large chunks*

1 red onion, *cut into large chunks*

3 garlic cloves

2 tomatoes on the vine *(or 3 plum tomatoes), finely diced*

¼ cup fresh parsley leaves, *chopped*

2 Tbsp olive oil

3 Tbsp tomato paste

3 Tbsp lemon juice

1 tsp cumin

1 tsp coriander

1 tsp salt

⅛-1 tsp crushed red pepper *(depending on how spicy you like it)*

2-3 packets sweetener

calories
8 calories per tablespoon

shani taub exchange
Free

[1] Place peppers into a food processor. Pulse 2-3 times to chop finely. Remove to a bowl. Add red onion and garlic to the processor; pulse 2-3 times to chop finely. Add to bowl.

[2] Add tomatoes and parsley to bowl. Stir in olive oil, tomato paste, lemon juice, cumin, coriander, salt, crushed red pepper, and sweetener. May be enjoyed right away or cover and refrigerate overnight to allow flavors to meld.

[Make Ahead] Because the vegetables are fresh, this won't freeze well, but it will last a couple of weeks in the fridge.

[Shani Says] Many people feel deprived because they can't have the full-fat dips they love on Shabbos. But now they can enjoy a few tablespoons of any of these dip options without counting the calories.

We've been very good at taking the healthy things Hashem gives us and frying them ... turning them into something worse than a cake or cookie. When we eat cake, we take just a sliver. But people think when they turn to vegetables at a simchah or in a restaurant they're doing justice to their diets. But that cauliflower is deep fried! Vegetables can be just as enjoyable in their healthy form. ~Shani

(5-ingredients or less!)
Veggies

I don't want my veggie side dish to add tons of calories to my meal.
Nor do I want it to take too much time to prepare. -Victoria

Secrets
No Oil = Still Great Results

The Key to Your Best Simple Roasted Veggies

→ Roast your veggies on a firm baking sheet. Not a disposable. And not a baking pan. Disposable sheets don't maintain enough heat and the high sides of a baking pan trap steam — resulting in soggy veggies.

→ Spread them out. Roasting veggies don't like to be crowded. They should have their own space so heat can circulate around all the surfaces.

→ Use nonstick cooking spray generously. It doesn't only replace the oil; it also allows seasonings to stick.

→ Make it hot. Though I always roast veggies at 425°-450°F, when roasting without oil, I find that I get great results when the temperature is at the higher 450°F. Yes, quick and hot.

→ Keep it simple. Make it special. Choose one veggie of each color for a really beautiful dish (e.g., carrots or butternut squash or sweet potato + broccoli or asparagus + red onion + yellow tomatoes or yellow peppers + red peppers or tomatoes) ... or find variety within one color scheme (how many veggies of one color can you find?).

→ Different veggies need different roasting times. So what do you do to avoid using multiple baking sheets? Dice the veggies that need more time smaller and keep the quick-cooking veggies larger; e.g., small sweet potato cubes + larger eggplant chunks.

Garlic 'n Onion Rutabaga Fries

Yields 4 servings ▫ Pareve
Gluten-Free ▫ Low Carb ▫ Sugar-Free ▫ Whole30 ▫ Paleo

The rutabaga is a type of turnip; it's usually in season in the winter, though often I'm lucky enough to find them all year round. I love them as a replacement for potatoes when baking a lower-cal baked French fry because they taste sweet and starchy like a potato. I prepare this easy side often ... and while the adults appreciate the health-factor, all of us, kids included, enjoy the flavor of these fries.

1 (1½-2 lb) **rutabaga**   ¾-1 tsp **garlic powder**
1½-2 tsp **salt**   ¾-1 tsp **onion powder**

calories
60-70 calories
per serving

shani taub exchange
1 serving =
½ vegetable

[1] Preheat oven to 450°F. Line a baking sheet with foil; coat with nonstick cooking spray.

[2] To peel and slice the rutabaga, first slice off the top and the root end. Then, peel off the slippery waxy peel. Cut peeled rutabaga into thin slices; then cut into thin French fry-like sticks.

[3] Spread rutabaga fries on prepared baking sheet. Coat with nonstick cooking spray, then sprinkle with salt, garlic powder, and onion powder. Toss to distribute spices evenly, then lay fries in a single layer and spray again. Bake for 40 minutes, until edges of fries are dark and caramelized.

[Good to Know] The rutabaga skin is waxy and slippery. This root veggie is much easier to slice when the skin is peeled off first.

[Shani Says] Some vegetables, such as rutabagas and winter squashes, are starchier than others. Enjoy them as a vegetable serving once per week, or as a bread when having them more often.

Za'atar Eggplant Skewers

Yields 7 skewers ▫ Pareve

Gluten-Free ▫ Low Carb ▫ Sugar-Free ▫ Whole30 ▫ Paleo

Why ever fry eggplant when you can pack so much flavor into so few calories in a side dish like this?

1 medium eggplant, *cubed*　　**coarse black pepper,** *for sprinkling*

salt, *for sprinkling*　　**garlic powder,** *for sprinkling*

ZA'ATAR SPLASH

1 Tbsp vinegar　　**1-2 garlic cloves,** *crushed*

½ Tbsp za'atar spice　　**3 Tbsp chopped fresh parsley leaves**

2 Tbsp water

SPECIAL EQUIPMENT

wooden or metal skewers

calories
18 calories per skewer

shani taub exchange
1 vegetable
for the entire recipe

[1] Place eggplant cubes into a colander; sprinkle with salt. Let sit to sweat for 30 minutes over bowl or in the sink; rinse and dry. Thread eggplant cubes on skewers (if using a grill, it is advisable to soak the wooden skewers first), about 7 cubes each.

[2] Coat skewered eggplant with nonstick cooking spray; sprinkle with black pepper and garlic powder.

[3] Coat a grill pan with nonstick cooking spray; heat over medium-high heat. Add skewers and cook, about 2 minutes per side (there are 4 sides). Spray skewers again during cooking if they appear dry. Set aside.

[4] **Meanwhile, prepare the za'atar splash:** Whisk together vinegar, za'atar, water, and garlic.

[5] Sprinkle za'atar splash on eggplant; top with fresh parsley. Serve hot or at room temperature.

One-Pan Glazed Green Beans

Yields 4 (8-ounce) servings □ Pareve

Gluten-Free □ Low Carb □ Paleo (use coconut aminos instead of soy sauce)

When we were working on Everyday Secret Restaurant Recipes, *Leah Schapira told me that one of her friends kept asking for the recipe for the green beans at one particular Manhattan restaurant. Though I didn't ask for the recipe (I preferred a different dish there), I did finally get to taste the green beans during a visit soon after. And though I liked the smoky, charred flavor, I didn't like that they were doused in a sweet sauce that likely contained lots of sugar.*

2 lb green beans

1 Tbsp fresh minced ginger
(or 3 frozen cubes)

2 Tbsp soy OR tamari sauce

2 tsp sesame oil

2 tsp honey

1 tsp salt, *plus to taste*

pinch coarse black pepper

calories
100 calories per serving

shani taub exchange
½ vegetable

GARNISHES

crushed red pepper flakes
(optional, for additional heat)

½ tsp sesame seeds

[1] Place ¼-inch water into a sauté pan; heat over medium-high heat until steam rises from the pan. Add green beans, cover, and steam for 3 minutes. Drain green beans; immediately rinse with cold water to stop the cooking process.

[2] Coat pan with nonstick cooking spray; return to high heat (the pan will already be hot). Add one layer of green beans (you will need to cook them in 2-3 batches) and cook until charred, about 90 seconds per side, or 3 minutes total, flipping halfway through.

[3] Meanwhile, in a small bowl, whisk together ginger, soy sauce, sesame oil, honey, salt, and pepper to create a sauce.

[4] When all beans have been charred, lower heat; return all beans to pan, add sauce, and stir to coat beans. Cook for 1 additional minute. Season with additional salt to taste.

No-Cal Sushi

Yields 5 (8-piece) rolls □ Pareve
Gluten-Free □ Sugar-Free □ Low Carb □ Whole30 □ Paleo

Well, almost. But if you're craving sushi but wish you could enjoy it without the carbs, this version totally satiates that craving and might even have some people fooled. Roll the nori tightly; using the whole nori sheet will help it remain sealed. Most of your sushi will stay together, though a few pieces might fall apart in the process. Don't serve those on your sushi platter; rather, they're perfect for taste-testing and munching. After all, they're (almost!) calorie-free!

"RICE"

1 *(24-oz)* **bag frozen cauliflower,** *partially thawed*

1½ tsp salt

1 Tbsp rice vinegar

FOR ASSEMBLY

5 nori sheets

vegetables AND/OR fish of your choice, *sliced into thin strips*

calories
44 calories per roll
(plus filling)

shani taub exchange
2 vegetables
for entire recipe

[1] Place cauliflower into a food processor. It should not be frozen solid, but still partly frozen, so it breaks apart nicely without getting mushy. Pulse cauliflower until pieces resemble grains of rice.

[2] Coat a sauté pan with nonstick cooking spray; heat over medium-high heat. Add cauliflower rice; cook, stirring occasionally, for 5 minutes, until cauliflower is cooked and moisture evaporates. Season with salt; stir in rice vinegar.

[3] Place a nori sheet on a sushi mat or paper towel in front of you. Pat cauliflower rice onto the bottom half of the nori in a thin layer. Spread filling across the center. Roll up the entire nori sheet (use the sushi mat or paper towel to help you), pressing to compress as you roll. Use a serrated knife to slice sushi. Serve alongside soy sauce and/or light spicy mayo.

[For the Family] Everyone enjoys sushi night in my house, with half the sushi made from rice and half made from cauli-rice. I prep a large assortment of julienned and thinly sliced veggies so everyone can choose what they want inside. It's sushi night — and the power of choice — that inspired my children to accept and try more and more vegetables.

[Try This!] Complete two dishes with one prep. Serve this with our Stir-Fry Over Salmon (page 228), and you can use the same veggies on your fish and inside your sushi.

[Shani Says] Use 3 ounces of fish in your sushi and enjoy this entire recipe as a complete meal.

Spaghetti Quiche

Yields 8 servings □ Pareve
Gluten-Free □ Low Carb □ Sugar-Free □ Whole30 □ Paleo

I love having those dishes on the Friday night table that I can just enjoy on the side without thinking about "how much." This is one that I prepare often. I bake it in a Pyrex dish and bring it directly to the table, but for a company-worthy healthy Shabbat side, dress it up by adding the basket-weave topping. And yes, you have permission to call this a kugel if you like.

1 *(2-3-lb)* **spaghetti squash**

1 large or 2 small onions, *thinly sliced*

1½ tsp salt, *or to taste, plus more for sprinkling*

2-3 lb zucchini, *julienned*

1 Tbsp fresh minced basil *(or 3 frozen cubes)*

6-8 egg whites *(depending on size of vegetables)*

OPTIONAL TOPPING

1 large zucchini, *thinly sliced on a mandoline*

salt, *for sprinkling*

garlic powder, *for sprinkling*

dried basil, *for sprinkling*

calories
59 calories per serving

shani taub exchange
2 servings = 1 vegetable

[1] Preheat oven to 400°F. Place whole spaghetti squash into oven; bake until all sides are soft and cave in slightly. Squash should be slightly golden. Let cool; cut in half and remove squash strands, discarding seeds and peel. Lower oven temperature to 350°F. (You can also soften the squash in the microwave.)

[2] Heat a sauté pan over medium-high heat. Coat with nonstick cooking spray, lower heat, add onions, and sprinkle with salt. Cover; cook, stirring occasionally, until soft, 5-7 minutes. Set aside.

[3] In a bowl, combine spaghetti squash, onion, zucchini, basil, salt, and egg whites. Add to a 9- x 13-inch baking dish or oval baking pan of similar size.

[4] To prepare the optional topping, place zucchini slices over the quiche in a basketweave pattern; sprinkle with salt, garlic powder, and dried basil.

[5] Bake for 1 hour, or until sides are golden and quiche appears set.

[Make Ahead] You can prepare and bake a day ahead and keep covered in the refrigerator. Warm before serving.

Zucchini Bruschetta

Yields 12-16 boats ▫ Pareve

Gluten-Free ▫ Low Carb ▫ Sugar-Free ▫ Whole30 ▫ Paleo

Following the birth of my first daughter, this was the side dish I prepared for Friday night during diet week number one. I wanted something that felt special and festive and was a fitting part of a Shabbat dinner, albeit super light. The recipe was given to me by a colleague, Chavi Sperber, who is a superbly talented cook, especially in the areas of preparing foods for those on special diets ... so she definitely knows how to extract flavor from simple ingredients, as she does here. The ingredient list may seem basic, but the first bite will really surprise you.

2 small or medium zucchini

2 garlic cloves, *crushed*

salt, *for sprinkling*

FILLING

2 cups grape tomatoes, *halved*

½ small red onion, *finely diced*

1 Tbsp balsamic vinegar

½ tsp dried basil

½ tsp salt

pinch coarse black pepper

calories
13 calories per boat

shani taub exchange
Complete recipe =
1 vegetable

[1]   Preheat oven to 400°F. Coat a baking sheet or pan with nonstick cooking spray.

[2]   Trim ends of zucchini; slice in half lengthwise. Using a spoon, scoop out the seeds and slice into 3-4 zucchini boats per half. Season zucchini with crushed garlic and salt. Place zucchini, cut side up, onto prepared baking sheet; bake for 20 minutes.

[3]   **Meanwhile, prepare the filling:** In a bowl, combine tomatoes, onion, vinegar, basil, salt, and pepper.

[4]   To serve, spoon filling into zucchini boats.

[Make Ahead] Prepare the boats and tomato salad up to a day ahead. Keep them separate. Warm the boats and add the tomato salad just before serving.

Thyme Roasted Autumn Vegetables

Yields 6 servings □ Pareve

Gluten-Free □ Low Carb □ Sugar-Free □ Whole30 □ Paleo

I originally intended to roast these vegetables to make a galette (a type of freeform pie). But then I found myself eating all the vegetables before they could make it onto the dough. So, I decided, this will be a vegetable dish that can stand on its own.

If you're purchasing pre-cut butternut squash, dice it even smaller so it will roast more quickly. But, if you shop in a market that sells all types of winter squashes, try something new. I love the flavor of delicata squash. It's also especially pretty, much easier to slice, and doesn't need to be peeled.

3 portobello mushroom caps, *sliced* **OR 6 ounces baby bella mushrooms,** *sliced*

1 tsp olive oil

1 Tbsp balsamic vinegar

1½ tsp salt, *divided*

1 delicata squash, *sliced into half-moons* **OR ½ butternut squash**, *peeled and diced*

2 pinches coarse black pepper, *divided*

1 *(24-oz)* **bag frozen cauliflower,** *thawed and drained*

1 red onion, *cut into rings*

1½ tsp dried thyme

calories
68 calories per serving

shani taub exchange
½ recipe = 1 vegetable

[1] In a small bowl, toss the mushrooms with olive oil and balsamic vinegar; sprinkle with ½ teaspoon salt. Set aside.

[2] Preheat oven to 425°F. Line two baking sheets with foil; coat with nonstick cooking spray. Divide squash between baking sheets, spray with nonstick cooking spray, and sprinkle with ½ teaspoon salt and pinch pepper. Bake for 15 minutes.

[3] Divide the cauliflower and red onion between the baking sheets. Spray entire mixture again; toss with thyme, remaining salt, and pepper. Bake for 20 minutes.

[4] Add reserved mushrooms (with the marinade) to the baking sheet; toss to mix with other vegetables. Bake for 10 additional minutes. Serve warm or at room temperature.

[Shani Says] We receive most of our vitamins and nutrients from vegetables, our lowest-calorie and most colorful foods. Find your favorite and fill up on it.

Roasted Silan Butternut Squash with Arugula

Yields 6 servings ▫ Pareve
Gluten-Free ▫ Low Carb

So here's why I love this dish. Though often the silan-roasted squash gets eaten directly off the baking sheet, the problem I have with roasted winter squash in general is the lack of variety in texture. It can be too mushy. This problem was solved when I paired it with the arugula and pomegranate seeds. A variety of dressings will work well here to flavor the greens, but these two are my favorites.

2 lbs cubed butternut squash
1 tsp salt
1 Tbsp silan
5 oz arugula

seeds of ½ pomegranate
¼ cup Tahini-Style Dressing *(page 232)* **OR Basil-Lime Vinaigrette** *(page 62)*

calories
163 calories per serving with Tahini-Style Dressing
143 calories per serving with Basil-Lime Vinaigrette

shani taub exchange
1 serving =
½ bread, ½ fruit

[1] Preheat oven to 450°F. Coat a baking sheet with nonstick cooking spray.

[2] Spread cubed squash on baking sheet. Coat squash with nonstick cooking spray. Sprinkle with salt; drizzle with silan. Toss to distribute; spread in an single layer. Bake for 20 minutes.

[3] To assemble, spread arugula on your platter or dish. Top with roasted squash, sprinkle with pomegranate seeds, and drizzle with dressing.

[Try This!] Turn any leftover squash into either version of butternut squash soup (pages 110-111) for the next day. You can supplement the roasted squash with additional fresh squash if you don't have enough.

[Good to Know] If you're starting with a whole butternut squash (rather than buying it pre-cubed), don't try to hack it with a knife to cube it. Rather, use the oven or microwave to soften it a bit so it's easy to peel and slice. Since you're roasting the squash, though, you don't want it to get soft. It should still be very firm when slicing.

Buttery Roasted Fennel and Pear

Yields 4 servings ▫ Pareve
Gluten-Free ▫ Low Carb ▫ Sugar-Free ▫ Whole30 ▫ Paleo

Nope, there's no butter in this dish. "Buttery" simply describes the texture of fennel and the magic that happens when this vegetable is roasted and transformed into something that's so distinct from its raw version. Enjoy something new and different without any extra effort! Though you can pair roasted fennel with lots of different veggies, it pairs especially well with roasted apples or pears. I chose red pears for the color contrast they bring to the dish.

2 fennel bulbs, *fronds removed, sliced*
1 red pear, *sliced*

1 tsp salt
¼ tsp coarse black pepper
½ tsp dried dill

calories
61 calories per serving

shani taub exchange
¼ vegetable, ¼ fruit

[1] Preheat oven to 425°F. Line a baking sheet with parchment paper or foil. If using foil, spray with nonstick cooking spray.

[2] Spread fennel and pear on prepared baking sheet; season with salt, pepper, and dill. Toss to combine; lay in a single layer. Bake for 25-30 minutes, or until fennel is soft.

Smoky Sweet Potato Fries

Yields 2 serving   ▫   Pareve

Smoked paprika just might be my favorite spice right now. And while I previously loved cumin on my sweet potato, this trumps it. I like serving sweet potato fries as a side dish because they're not "trying" to be French fries. We love them for their own flavor that they bring to the table. I do find that sweet potato fries, unlike the other vegetables in this book, need a little oil to bake properly.

2 sweet potatoes, *sliced into sticks*   **½ tsp onion powder**

2 tsp smoked paprika   **4 tsp oil**

½ tsp chili powder   **1 tsp salt**

½ tsp garlic powder

calories
225 calories per serving

shani taub exchange
1 bread per
4 ounces potato

[1]   Preheat oven to 450°F. Coat a baking sheet with nonstick cooking spray.

[2]   In a small bowl, combine paprika, chili powder, garlic powder, and onion powder. Toss sweet potatoes with oil and spices. Spread in a single layer on baking sheet; coat with nonstick cooking spray. Bake for 20 minutes, until dark at the edges; season with salt.

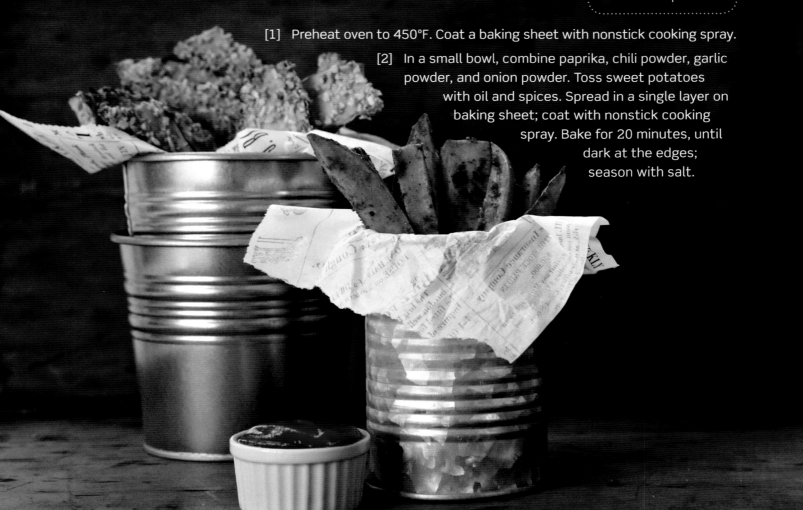

Crispy Sticks

Yields 2 serving □ Pareve

Did you ever think that it was possible to enjoy a crispy breading without adding calories to a dish? Use only fresh vegetables with this technique, as frozen vegetables have too much moisture and the "breading" won't crisp up.

CHOICE OF VEGETABLES

1 small eggplant, *sliced into sticks, salted, rinsed, and dried*
OR 1½ lb asparagus, *trimmed* **OR ¼ kabocha squash** *(or favorite winter squash), sliced into sticks*

COATING

2 egg whites, *beaten*   **2 tsp salt**

6 Tbsp dried minced onion   **pinch coarse black pepper**

6 Tbsp dried minced garlic

> calories
> 73-81 calories
> per serving
>
> shani taub exchange
> 1 vegetable

[1]   Preheat oven to 450°F. Coat a baking sheet with nonstick cooking spray.

[2]   Place beaten egg whites into a bowl. In a second bowl, combine minced onion, minced garlic, salt, and pepper. Pour half of mixture onto a plate (this is so the mixture doesn't clump up and become unusable).

[3]   Dip vegetables into egg white; dredge in onion/garlic mixture, pressing so that mixture sticks to the surface. Place on prepared baking sheet. Add more onion/garlic mixture to plate as needed.

[4]   Bake asparagus and eggplant for 20 minutes; bake winter squash for 25 minutes, until onion/garlic coating is crisp and golden. Serve immediately.

[Good to Know] The onion/garlic coating is only crispy when fresh! Don't crowd them in a pan or cover them, even after baking, or they'll become soggy.

[Shani Says] Try kabocha squash! It's a winter squash that looks like a green pumpkin, but has half the carbs of butternut and ⅓ fewer calories. The skin is edible once roasted, so skip the peeling.

Zoodles with Bolognese Sauce

Yields 4 servings □ Pareve

This is the only recipe in this chapter with more than five ingredients. Unlike the other recipes, though, it's not a side dish (though it can be). This all-veggie dish feels like a meal ... a filling "meaty" dish without many calories at all. This recipe arose from my fleish-phobia (fear of eating meat and then not being able to eat dairy for 6 hours). Now I can have the satisfaction of a hearty meat sauce ... with no worries of having eaten meat. Hey, I can even sprinkle some Parm on top (that'll make it dairy, of course).

4 large or 6 medium zucchini or yellow squash, *julienned*

salt, *for sprinkling*

pinch coarse black pepper

2 garlic cloves, *crushed*

BOLOGNESE SAUCE

1 onion, *diced*

3 garlic cloves, *crushed*

1 tsp salt,
plus more for sprinkling

2 carrots, *peeled and diced*

2 celery stalks, *diced*

20 oz baby bella mushrooms,
finely diced

4 oz shiitake mushrooms,
finely diced

½ tsp dried thyme

½ tsp dried oregano

½ cup red wine

1 *(15-oz)* **can tomato sauce**

> calories
> 154 calories per serving
>
> shani taub exchange
> 1 vegetable

[1] **Prepare the sauce:** Coat a large sauté pan with nonstick cooking spray; heat over medium heat. Add onion and garlic; season with salt. Cover, lower heat, and cook for 5 minutes. Add carrots and celery; cook an additional 3-5 minutes.

[2] Add mushrooms; cook over low heat until mushrooms shrink and are deeply browned, about 20-24 minutes. Season with salt, thyme, and oregano.

[3] Add red wine; cook for 2-3 minutes to let alcohol evaporate. Add tomato sauce; cook until sauce thickens, about 10 minutes.

[4] **Prepare the zoodles:** Toss zucchini with salt, pepper, and garlic. Microwave for 3 minutes; divide between 4 bowls. Top with Bolognese sauce; serve.

Soups
(the low-cal comfort food)

Never stuffed, never hungry ... but always satisfied. That's how I want my clients to feel. I don't introduce soups into my clients' diets until the second week. Chewing food sends a message to the brain that you actually ate, so I want them to have the most satisfying foods that first week ... they should actually eat their veggies and drink their water. After that ... enjoy those soups as a warm, nourishing way to get your veggies. -Shani

Roasted Mushroom and Eggplant Soup

Yields 4 (1¾-cup) servings □ Pareve
Gluten-Free □ Sugar-Free □ Low Carb □ Whole30 □ Paleo

My family is not particularly big into soups. Those purees of zucchini don't really do it for us … and I tried lots of variations when testing options for this book. For a soup to be cookbook worthy, it had to be one that even non soup-lovers would love. This was one combination that we instantly loved and now repeatedly finish down to the bottom of the pot. Don't skip the step of salting the eggplant; without that step, your soup will be bitter.

1 eggplant, *peeled and diced*

2 tsp salt, *or to taste, plus more for sprinkling*

24 oz sliced baby bella mushrooms

1 onion, *sliced*

6 garlic cloves

5 cups water

⅛ tsp coarse black pepper

calories
85 calories per serving

shani taub exchange
1 vegetable

[1] Place diced eggplant into a colander. Sprinkle with salt; let sit over a bowl or in the sink for 20-30 minutes to sweat. Rinse and dry.

[2] Meanwhile, preheat oven to 425°F. Coat 2 baking sheets with nonstick cooking spray. Spread eggplant, mushrooms, onion, and garlic on baking sheets. Coat with nonstick cooking spray; roast for 20 minutes.

[3] Transfer contents of baking sheets to a pot. Add water; bring to a boil. Lower heat; simmer for 45 minutes. Transfer contents of pot in batches to a blender and blend until smooth (or use an immersion blender right in the pot). Season with salt and pepper.

Maple & Cinnamon Butternut Squash Soup

Yields 7 (1 cup) servings ▫ Pareve
Gluten-Free ▫ Low Carb ▫ Paleo

Sure, you can make a great butternut squash soup without adding a sweetener. I don't mind a little bit, though, because it's precisely that flavor that makes this feel more indulgent than it is. If my whole family considers this veggie a treat, I'll take it.

1 *(3-lb)* **butternut squash**
(yields 2 lb flesh)
1 large onion, *chopped*
1½ tsp salt, *or to taste*
5 cups water, *or as needed*

2 Tbsp maple syrup OR silan
½ tsp cinnamon
silan, *optional garnish*
slivered almonds,
optional garnish

calories
97 calories per cup
(without garnish)

shani taub exchange
1 bread

[1]   Preheat oven to 400°F. Place whole butternut squash into oven; bake until golden and soft on all sides, about 1 hour. Remove from oven.

[2]   Meanwhile, coat the bottom of a large pot with nonstick cooking spray. Heat over medium high heat. Add onion, sprinkle with salt, cover, and let cook until soft, 5-7 minutes. Set aside

[3]   When squash is cool enough to handle, remove peel and seeds. Add flesh to pot. Add water to cover. Bring to a boil, lower heat, and simmer for 35-45 minutes. Transfer soup, in batches, to a blender and blend until smooth (or use an immersion blender right in the pot).

[4]   Return soup to pot; season with salt. Stir in maple syrup and cinnamon. Optional garnish: sprinkle with almonds and add a swirl of silan, as pictured (facing page).

[Try This!] Have leftover Silan Butternut Squash (page 98)? Simply add it to this soup in Step 3.

Butternut Squash and Red Lentil Soup

Yields 12 (¾ cup) servings ▫ Pareve

Gluten-Free ▫ Sugar-Free ▫ Low Carb ▫ Whole30 ▫ Paleo

Soup season seems to always begin on the first night of Sukkot. That's the night when my extended family sits down to a choice of two new heartwarming soups. One year, this was a combination that a sister-in-law introduced to us, and it became instantly popular for its heartiness and Middle Eastern flair.

1 *(3-lb)* **butternut squash**
(yields 2 lb flesh)

1 large onion, *chopped*

2 tsp salt, *or to taste, plus more for sprinkling*

1 cup red lentils

7 cups water

1 tsp cumin, *plus more for optional garnish*

1 tsp coriander

pinch coarse black pepper

pine nuts, *optional garnish*

calories
97 calories per serving
(without garnish)

shani taub exchange
1 bread

[1]   Preheat oven to 400°F. Place whole butternut squash into oven; bake until golden and soft on all sides, about 1 hour. Remove from oven.

[2]   Meanwhile, coat the bottom of a large pot with nonstick cooking spray. Heat over medium high heat. Add onion, sprinkle with salt, cover, and let cook until soft, 5-7 minutes.

[3]   When squash is cool enough to handle, remove peel and seeds. Add flesh to pot. Add red lentils and water. Bring to a boil, lower heat, and simmer for 30 minutes. Transfer soup, in batches, to a blender and blend until smooth (or use an immersion blender right in the pot).

[4]   Return soup to pot; season with 2 teaspoons salt. Add cumin, coriander, and black pepper. Optional garnish: sprinkle with cumin and pine nuts (as pictured).

Maple & Cinnamon
Butternut Squash Soup
↓

Butternut Squash and ↗
Red Lentil Soup

Soups

Cream of Celery
Root and Onion Soup
↙ (page 114)

Cream of Celery Root and Onion Soup

Yields 4 (1-cup) servings ▫ Pareve
Gluten-Free ▫ Sugar-Free ▫ Low Carb ▫ Whole30 ▫ Paleo

You can imagine that I roasted, simmered, and blended lots of vegetables to find the best purees for this book. Celery root was one of my favorite discoveries that led to a finish-the-pot moment. When blended, it has the silkiness (though not the calories) of a potato, with hints of celery flavor. I had just one dilemma: The white puree was so beautiful, but I found when I caramelized the onion and sautéed the celery root with it until both were golden, the result was so irresistible that we often ate those celery chunks before they even made it to the blending stage. The choice is yours: add the root and water before onions turn golden for a beautiful white soup, or caramelize it all.

Since celery roots come in all sizes, to keep the right proportions measure your cubes and use 1 onion for every 2 cups of diced celery root.

2 onions, *diced*
(see note in intro above)
salt, *to taste, plus more for sprinkling*

4 cups diced celery root
4 cups water
pinch white pepper

calories
85 calories per cup

shani taub exchange
1 vegetable

[1] Coat the bottom of a large pot with nonstick cooking spray. Heat over medium high heat. Add onions, sprinkle with salt, and cover. Cook, stirring occasionally, until onions are completely soft, about 10 minutes.

[2] Add celery root; cover with water. Bring to a boil, lower heat, and simmer for 45 minutes. Transfer contents to a blender and blend until smooth (or use an immersion blender right in the pot). Return to pot; season with salt and pepper.

Churba Soup

Yields 4 servings   □   Meat
Gluten-Free   □   Sugar-Free   □   Low Carb

This is the comforting soup of my childhood memories; the Syrian answer to chicken-and-matzah ball soup. Though there are lots of variations of Churba, this is the way I remember it. While I was reminiscing about this soup, I realized it could be perfect for this book too. How else does one little quarter-cup of rice expand to fill an entire pot? It seems like magic ... and though this will yield a generous four bowls of soup, you could essentially make the entire pot into a meal (though I think you'll be full long before you finish it). The entire pot is 388 calories, and you're getting rice and chicken!

1 bone-in chicken breast

¼ cup rice

2 plum tomatoes, *quartered,* **OR 1 large beefsteak tomato,** *cut into eighths*

4 celery ribs, *trimmed*

6 cups chicken stock

salt, *to taste*

calories
97 calories
per serving
. . . .
shani taub exchange
½ bread, ½ protein
per serving

[1] In a medium pot, combine chicken, rice, tomatoes, celery, and chicken stock. Bring to a boil; lower heat and simmer for 2 hours. Soup will take on a creamy, thick consistency and vegetables will seem wilted.

[2] Remove chicken breast from soup; shred chicken. Return shredded chicken to pot. Taste and season with salt, if necessary, before serving.

[Shani Says] During maintenance, you can have this entire pot as 2 breads and 2 proteins.

Veggie Miso Soup

Yields 5 servings □ Pareve
Gluten-Free □ Sugar-Free □ Low Carb

This is a satiating feel-good soup I've been making for years as an accompaniment to any Asian-style dinner. And, unlike other soups that often need long simmering time, this one gets its flavor at the end from the miso paste, so it's ready fairly quickly. If you love miso, but aren't into tofu and seaweed, this is the solution.

3 garlic cloves, *crushed*
2 tsp minced fresh ginger
(or 2 frozen cubes)
4 oz fresh baby spinach
1 zucchini, *chopped*

1 carrot, *julienned*
2 cups sliced mushrooms
1 *(15-oz)* **can baby corn,** *drained*
¼ cup dark miso paste
2 Tbsp salt

calories
79 calories per serving

shani taub exchange
1 vegetable

[1] In a large pot, combine garlic, ginger, spinach, zucchini, carrot, mushrooms, and baby corn. Add water to cover. Bring to a boil; lower heat and simmer for 20 minutes.

[2] Stir in miso paste (to make it easier to blend in, you can optionally first combine the miso paste with some broth to thin it). Season with salt; serve.

[Shani Says] Vegetables in soups hold on to salt more than vegetables in a salad would, so they might cause bloating. But don't worry; any weight gain that results isn't real. It will only be temporary.

Green Goodness
↙ Soup

Green Goodness Soup

Yields 6 (1-cup) servings □ Pareve or Meat

I've blended a lot of stuff in this chapter, but not a zucchini or cauliflower. I really tried to give you some unique flavors that aren't already in your repertoire of light soups. My blender was busy as I tested all those different combinations. It could finally rest once I combined these "green" ingredients.

1 onion, *diced*

2 garlic cloves, *crushed*

1 fennel bulb, *fronds removed, sliced*

1 lb asparagus, *tips, leaves, and white ends removed, divided*

2-3 oz *(about 2 large handfuls)* **fresh baby spinach**

4 cups vegetable OR chicken stock

1½ tsp salt, *or to taste*

calories
38 calories per cup
- - - - - - - - -
shani taub exchange
2 cups = 1 vegetable

[1] Heat a medium saucepan with nonstick cooking spray. Add onion and garlic; sauté over low heat for about 5 minutes. Add fennel and ¾ of the asparagus; cook an additional 2 minutes.

[2] Add spinach; stir until spinach begins to wilt. Add stock; bring to a boil. Lower heat; simmer for 20 minutes. In a blender or using an immersion blender, blend most of the soup, leaving a few chunks.

[3] Dice remaining asparagus. Heat a sauté pan coated with nonstick cooking spray. Sauté asparagus until edges are golden. Add sautéed asparagus to each bowl of soup.

[Try This!] For dairy meals, be sure to use vegetable stock; you can add protein to these soups by garnishing with a dollop or swirl of Greek yogurt, as pictured.

Basil Soup
with Carrots
and Tomatoes ↗

Basil Soup
with Carrots and Tomatoes

Yields 2 servings □ Pareve or Meat

One major pet peeve lots of people have about tomato soups is that they taste like marinara sauce. This isn't such a bad thing; after all, most people like marinara. My kids love the "Pizza Soup" in Kids Cooking Made Easy, *which is essentially sauce with milk. Some need their soup to taste different. To create a tomato-based soup that doesn't taste like sauce, I skipped the cans and roasted lots of veggies and herbs. If you're serving this right away, this one barely even needs a pot!*

4 Roma or plum tomatoes, *quartered*

2 carrots, *peeled and diced*

1 onion, *diced*

3 garlic cloves

½ red pepper, *cut into chunks*

1 tsp salt, *plus more to taste*

pinch coarse black pepper

1 tsp dried basil

1 tsp dried thyme

1 tsp dried oregano

1½ cups vegetable OR chicken stock

1 Tbsp fresh minced basil

calories
75 calories per serving

shani taub exchange
1 vegetable
for entire recipe

[1] Preheat oven to 425°F. Line a baking sheet with parchment paper; coat with nonstick cooking spray.

[2] On the baking sheet, toss tomatoes, carrots, onion, garlic, and red pepper with salt, pepper, basil, thyme, and oregano. Bake for 35 minutes.

[3] Transfer contents of baking sheet to a blender. Add stock and fresh basil; blend to combine. Season with additional salt, if desired, to taste. Enjoy immediately or transfer to a pot to keep warm.

I'm not anti-carb in any way. Often, people come to me after they've been eating only proteins and vegetables for a while. There's a misconception that they'll lose weight that way. But a low-fat carb is often better than a high-fat protein. The only difference is the absorbency. Pour water on a fatty piece of meat. There's no absorbency. Now pour it over a fat-free cereal. The cereal will grow and absorb the water. When people eliminate carbs, they lose water weight, not fat or calories. The minute they take carbs into their bodies, though, they'll gain it back. If someone takes in the right amount of proteins and carbs in moderation, though, that person will lose fat and calories and the weight will stay off forever. -Shani

Friendly Carbs

(fun appetizers,
whole grains
& sandwiches)

Secrets
How to Stretch a Grain

One night, I prepared two different side dishes for my husband. In one bowl, was
½ cup brown rice tossed with cucumber, tomato, fresh parsley, lemon juice, and spices.
I wasn't sure how he'd take to this Israeli-salad style of rice, so in a second bowl I
placed ½ cup plain brown rice. When I served dinner, I presented him with both options.

"Which one do you want?" I asked.

"That one ... it's much more!" he said, pointing to the Israeli-style brown rice.

You know, it wasn't much more. It just seemed that way.

So that's how we stretch the grain.

When a grain is "stretched," the result isn't only fewer calories or a bigger portion.
You get more flavor and enjoyment, too.

-Victoria

Veggie Egg Rolls

Yields 10 spring rolls   □   Pareve
Sugar-Free

I use spring roll wrappers here, rather than egg roll wrappers, because they don't need to be fried … they're crispy and delectable even when baked (they're also lower in calories, of course!). The secret to a perfect stir-fry filling is to cook the vegetables in small batches over high heat, so they get nice caramelization and stay crisp. If you want to double the recipe, cook each batch of vegetables separately. You can sub veggies as long as the overall quantity is the same; slice thinly so they cook quickly.

1 Tbsp sesame oil
1 onion, *thinly sliced*
1 garlic clove, *crushed*
1 tsp minced fresh ginger
2 carrots, *peeled and julienned*

1 zucchini, *cut into matchsticks*
½ cup sugar snap peas, *halved vertically*
1 Tbsp soy sauce
½ tsp salt, *or to taste*
10 spring roll wrappers

calories
55 calories
per spring roll

shani taub exchange
½ bread, ⅒ vegetable

[1] Preheat oven to 350°F. Line a baking sheet with parchment paper or foil; coat with nonstick cooking spray.

[2] Heat a wok or sauté pan over high heat until very hot. Add sesame oil, onion, garlic, and ginger; cook for 2 minutes, stirring constantly. Add carrots and zucchini; cook for an additional 2 minutes. Add sugar snap peas; cook for 1 more minute. Stir in soy sauce; season with salt, if needed. Let cool.

[3] Lay a spring roll wrapper in front of you. Add filling along the center, toward the bottom. Brush edges with water. Fold up bottom to cover filling. Fold in sides; roll up wrapper. Place on prepared baking sheet. Repeat with remaining wrappers and filling.

[4] Coat filled wrappers with nonstick cooking spray. Bake until golden and crispy, 13-15 minutes.

[Good to Know] Here's an easy way to julienne a carrot: Place the peeled carrot on your cutting board. Pierce the stem end with a fork and hold the carrot in place by pressing down on the fork handle. Then simply julienne using your julienne peeler.

[Make Ahead] If you choose to freeze these, defrost completely before baking. If you bake straight from the freezer, the outside will crisp before the inside defrosts.

Nachos

Yields 4 servings   □   Pareve
Sugar-Free

Nachos are so much fun to eat — take a chip, pile on the toppings! Every bite is exciting. This is especially amazing in the summertime, when tomatoes and corn are naturally sweet. I used 80-calorie wraps to make the chips. Although round wraps are more accessible, I find that square wraps crisp up into a more substantial, thicker "chip."

CHIPS

3 low-calorie wraps
garlic powder, *for sprinkling*

salt, *for sprinkling*
chili powder, *for sprinkling*

PICO DE GALLO

2 cups chopped tomatoes
2 Tbsp lime juice

kernels from 2 ears cooked fresh corn
1 Tbsp red wine vinegar

½ small red onion, *finely diced*
1 tsp salt

½-1 jalapeno, *seeds and membranes discarded, finely diced*
pinch coarse black pepper

AVOCADO-CUCUMBER CREAM

1 ripe avocado
3 Tbsp lime juice

½ cucumber, *peeled*
½ tsp salt

2 tsp cilantro *(OR 2 frozen cubes)*

> calories
> 143 calories for 8 chips,
> 1 serving pico de gallo,
> and 2 Tbsp Avocado-
> Cucumber Cream
>
> shani taub exchange
> 1 bread,
> ¼ vegetable, 1 fat

[1] **Prepare the chips:** Preheat oven to 400°F. Line a baking sheet with parchment paper. Using a pizza slicer, slice each wrap into about 10 tortilla-shaped triangles. Spread on prepared baking sheet, coat with nonstick cooking spray. Sprinkle with salt, garlic powder, and chili powder. Bake until golden and crisp, 7-8 minutes.

[2] **Prepare the pico de gallo:** In a bowl, stir together tomatoes, corn kernels, red onion, jalapeno, lime juice, vinegar, salt, and pepper.

[3] **Prepare the avocado-cucumber cream:** Using a blender, combine avocado, cucumber, cilantro, lime juice, and salt. You may need to add up to 1 tablespoon water to start the blending process.

[4] To enjoy, scoop up some Pico de Gallo with a chip and top with a dollop of Avocado-Cucumber Cream.

[Shani Says] People often ask, "How can I host a party while dieting and still feel like I'm part of it?" This is one way to enjoy finger foods and have fun.

Shirataki Lo Mein

Yields 1 large serving □ Pareve
Gluten-Free □ Low Carb

As with egg rolls, you can use whatever stir-fry vegetables (such as sugar snap peas), you have in your fridge here, but slice them thinly so they cook quickly. This ENTIRE portion is 146 calories.

Shirataki noodles are made from a Japanese yam that happens to be virtually calorie-free (the final product has a minimal number of calories). They're tasteless and colorless, so whether they taste good depends on what you do with them. Shirataki noodles are available in the refrigerated section near the tofu in mainstream supermarkets.

1 *(6-ounce)* **package shirataki spaghetti**
1 carrot, *julienned*
½ cup shredded red cabbage

1 oz sliced mushrooms
½ tsp salt, *or to taste*
scallions, *for garnish,*

calories
146 calories

shani taub exchange
1 vegetable

SAUCE
2 tsp soy sauce
1 tsp sesame oil
1 tsp sugar

1 tsp rice vinegar
2 garlic cloves, *minced*
1 tsp fresh minced ginger, *optional*

[1] Drain and rinse shirataki noodles.

[2] **Prepare the sauce:** In a small bowl, combine all sauce ingredients.

[3] Heat a wok or sauté pan over high heat. Add noodles and "dry-fry" until the pan is steaming and liquid completely evaporates (there should not be any water left in the pan when the other ingredients are added or it will dilute the flavor).

[4] Add carrot, cabbage, and mushrooms; cook over high heat for 1-2 minutes until veggies are crisp-tender.

[5] Add sauce; stir until sauce thickens and coats all noodles. Season with salt to taste. Add scallions.

Crispy Eggplant Wontons
with Two Dipping Sauces

Yields 36 wontons   □   Pareve
Sugar-Free

You're going to see this Tahini-Style Dressing used in this book again. And again. And, yup, once more. I'll tell you why: I didn't write this book to show how many recipes I could create. I wrote this book to give you practical solutions for everyday life. And while we might love techina, it's very calorie-dense. This dressing captures its essence at a fraction of the calories. So if you have a jar in your fridge that you can use as a dip (here), with your side dish (Roasted Silan Butternut Squash, page 98), on a salad, or in a wrap (The Sabich, page 142), or on your fish (Techina Salmon, page 232), well, that just makes life easier!

36 round wonton wrappers   **oregano,** *for sprinkling*

garlic powder, *for sprinkling*   **za'atar,** *for sprinkling*

basil, *for sprinkling*   **cumin,** *for sprinkling*

EGGPLANT PUREE
1 eggplant   **2 tsp lemon juice**

2 garlic cloves   **1 tsp salt**

FOR SERVING
marinara sauce, *warmed,* **AND/OR Tahini-Style Dressing** *(page 232)*

calories
24 calories per wonton

shani taub exchange
4 wontons = 1 bread

[1] **Prepare eggplant puree:** Place eggplant over an open flame set to medium heat. Cook eggplant until each side is soft and collapsed, about 5 minutes per side or 20 minutes total.

[2] Let eggplant cool; peel off and discard skin. Transfer eggplant flesh to a food processor or blender. Add garlic, lemon juice, and salt; blend to combine.

[3] Meanwhile, preheat oven to 425°F. Coat a baking sheet with nonstick cooking spray.

[4] **Assemble the wontons:** Place one teaspoon eggplant puree in the center of each wonton wrapper. Using a pastry brush, brush the edges of each wrapper with water; fold edges together and press to seal. Place wontons on prepared baking sheet. Sprinkle with garlic powder. Sprinkle half the wontons with basil and oregano, and the other half with za'atar and cumin (or choose the flavor profile you prefer). Bake for 11-13 minutes, until edges are brown and crisp.

[5] Serve basil-oregano wontons alongside marinara sauce. Serve za'atar-cumin wontons alongside Tahini-Style Dressing.

[Make Ahead] Wontons can be frozen either baked or raw.

Rice and Leben

Yields 4 servings ☐ Dairy
Gluten-Free ☐ Sugar-Free

I love when I take a bite of something and think, "Oh wow. I wasn't expecting it to be that good." We might not expect some combinations to work. But they do anyway. Both my husband and I grew up enjoying rice with yogurt or sour cream. It's a traditional, comforting combination. The addition of the veggie salad, transforming it into a colorful and more filling dish, makes it even better.

⅔ cup brown or white rice   **salt,** *to taste*
1 onion, *diced*

VEGGIE TOPPING

2 large fresh *(golden or candy cane, if available)* **beets OR ready-cooked vacuum-sealed beets** *(not canned)*

¼ English cucumber OR 1 Persian cucumber, *finely diced*

¾ cup grape tomatoes, *finely diced*

½ Tbsp good-quality balsamic vinegar

1 tsp salt

calories
211 calories per serving

shani taub exchange
1 bread, ¼ vegetable

CUCUMBER LEBEN

1 *(6-oz)* **container plain Greek yogurt OR plain Leben**

¼ English cucumber OR 1 Persian cucumber, *grated or finely diced*

½ tsp salt

[1] Prepare rice according to package instructions.

[2] Skip this step if using vacuum-sealed beets. Preheat oven to 425°F. Wrap beets in foil. Place in oven and roast until soft, 45 minutes-1 hour. Let cool; peel and dice beets.

[3] In a bowl, combine diced beets, cucumber, tomatoes, balsamic vinegar, and salt. Set aside.

[4] Heat a sauté pan over medium-high heat. Lower heat, coat pan with nonstick cooking spray, add onion, and sprinkle with salt. Cover and cook, stirring occasionally, until golden, about 20 minutes. You can uncover the pan after about 7 minutes when there is enough moisture in the pan.

[5] **Prepare the leben:** Combine yogurt, cucumber, and salt in a small bowl.

[6] Add caramelized onion to rice; season with salt to taste. To serve, top rice with veggie topping and drizzle leben on top.

Roasted Mushroom and Shallot Rice

Yields 3 servings □ Meat
Gluten-Free □ Sugar-Free

If you keep the mushrooms whole (here's your chance to use all those cool varieties you see in the super-market), the roasted shallots and mushrooms even work well on their own as a side dish. Don't substitute the shallots for another type of onion. The little guys caramelize beautifully, even without oil, and are my favorite bites in this dish.

16 oz assorted mushrooms *(use at least 3 varieties, including shiitake, oyster, baby bella, or white button), large ones halved*

6 large shallots, *peeled*

1 tsp dried thyme

2 garlic cloves, *crushed*

1½ tsp salt, *plus more to taste*

pinch coarse black pepper

½ cup wild rice

chicken OR beef stock, *for cooking rice*

1 Tbsp balsamic vinegar

1 cup arugula or spring greens *(optional)*

calories
164 calories per serving

shani taub exchange
1 bread, ½ vegetable

[1]   Preheat oven to 425°F. Spread mushrooms on a baking sheet. Separate shallots into segments (you can halve any that are very large); place on baking sheet. Sprinkle with thyme, garlic, salt, and pepper; coat with nonstick cooking spray. Toss to coat ingredients evenly; spread in an even layer. Coat again with nonstick cooking spray. Roast for 25 minutes.

[2]   Meanwhile, prepare rice in a small saucepan according to package instructions, using the stock as the liquid.

[3]   Toss warm rice and mushroom mixture with balsamic vinegar and greens (if using); season with additional salt to taste; serve warm.

[Good to Know] To make this dish pareve, use veggie stock or pareve chicken- or beef-flavored stock.

Better-with-Veggies Spanish Rice

Yields 6 servings   □   Pareve
Gluten-Free   □   Sugar-Free

If I told you it was possible to have a rice side dish that's way more satisfying than just plain rice ... and you could have double the portion ... and that double portion was still fewer calories than a regular ½-cup serving of rice ... it would be too good to be true, right? But it is true!

1 onion, *diced*

3 garlic cloves, *crushed*

1 tsp salt, *plus more for sprinkling*

1 cup rice

1 tsp cumin

2 tsp chili powder

1 *(15-ounce)* **can diced tomatoes with their liquid**

1¼ cups water

1 lb mini peppers, *stems removed, sliced into rings*

3 carrots, *peeled and diced*

8 oz broccoli florets, *sliced*

calories
182 calories per serving

shani taub exchange
¾ bread, ½ vegetable

[1]   Coat a large sauté pan or saucepan with nonstick cooking spray; heat over medium-high heat. Lower heat; add onion and garlic, sprinkle with salt, cover, and cook until onion is soft, 5-7 minutes.

[2]   Add rice; stir to toast for 1 minute. Stir in cumin, chili powder, and 1 teaspoon salt. Add diced tomatoes and water.

[3]   Bring to a boil; lower heat, cover, and simmer until rice is cooked, 15 minutes. Stir occasionally so the rice cooks evenly.

[4]   Meanwhile, coat a large sauté pan with nonstick cooking spray and heat over high heat. Add peppers, carrots, and broccoli; stir-fry for 5 minutes, until cooked but still crisp. Season with salt to taste. Stir into the rice during the last few minutes of cooking.

[Try This!] Serve this next to a bowl of Mushroom Chili (page 214)
for a heartwarming and satiating meal.

Ramen Bowl

Yields 2 servings □ Pareve or Meat

I never tried instant noodle soup until the Fat Free Low Sodium versions came on the market. Though they still aren't considered healthy, at 186 calories, they're a filling and basic mini meal. But why settle for freeze-dried veggies and chicken consommé powder when you can enjoy those comforting noodles in a bright, colorful, and naturally flavorful dish? Enjoy this as a noodle side dish, or add the chicken strips for a complete meal.

2 oz Ramen noodles
1 carrot, *julienned*
1 cup mushrooms, *thinly sliced*

1 cup shredded red cabbage
2 cups fresh baby spinach

DRESSING

¼ cup soy sauce
¼ cup orange juice
2 Tbsp lime juice

2 tsp minced fresh ginger
(or 2 cubes frozen)
1 Tbsp sesame oil

CHICKEN (OPTIONAL)

2 skinless, boneless chicken breasts, *thinly sliced*
salt, *for sprinkling*

black pepper, *for sprinkling*
2 garlic cloves, *crushed*

calories
232 calories per serving
add 150 calories
per serving with chicken

shani taub exchange
1 bread, 2 proteins,
½ vegetable, ½ fat
per serving

[1] Soak noodles in hot water for 4 minutes. Drain.

[2] Meanwhile, coat a sauté pan with nonstick cooking spray; heat over high heat. Add carrot and mushrooms; sauté for 2 minutes. Set aside.

[3] **Prepare the dressing:** In a bowl, whisk together soy sauce, orange juice, lime juice, ginger, and sesame oil.

[4] If including chicken, season with salt, pepper, and garlic. Add 2 spoons of dressing; marinate for a few minutes or up to overnight. Heat a sauté pan coated with nonstick cooking spray. Add chicken; cook 3-4 minutes per side. Remove from pan and slice into strips (if chicken is not cooked all the way through, return chicken strips to the pan and sauté quickly until cooked through).

[5] In a large bowl, arrange noodles, carrot-mushroom sauté, red cabbage, baby spinach, and chicken, if using, in different sections. Drizzle with dressing. Toss together when ready to eat. For a hot dish, you can also toss all the components together in a sauté pan and cook over high heat for 2 minutes, until sauce coats all ingredients.

Warm Roasted Garlic Farro

Yields 4 serving   □   Pareve

I think that lots of us want to learn how to cook the new, wholesome grains that are now available. We know rice, we know barley, we even know quinoa by now. But what do we do with farro? Or wheat berries? Both grains have a nutty taste and chewy texture. I enjoy them like rice ... warm and fresh. Serve this hot so the squash melts into the grain.

1 eggplant, *diced*
2 tsp salt, *plus more for sprinkling*
⅔ cup farro
2 zucchini, *diced*
12 garlic cloves

1 onion, *cut into strips*
pinch coarse black pepper
juice of 1 lemon *(3-4 Tbsp)*
½ cup fresh parsley leaves

calories
179 calories per serving

shani taub exchange
1 bread, ½ vegetable

[1] Place eggplant to a colander; sprinkle with salt. Let sit 20 minutes over a bowl or in the sink; rinse and pat dry.

[2] Preheat oven to 450°F.

[3] Prepare farro according to package instructions.

[4] On 2 baking sheets, toss eggplant, zucchini, garlic, and onion with salt and pepper. Coat with nonstick cooking spray. Roast for 20 minutes.

[5] Immediately toss hot roasted vegetables with farro. Season with salt and pepper to taste. Add lemon juice; toss with parsley before serving.

The Sabich

Yields 2 servings □ Pareve
Gluten-Free □ Sugar-Free

This is one of my absolute favorites, because there are so many ways you can enjoy it! The Sabich is typically a classic Israeli breakfast, including fried eggplant, Israeli salad, hard-boiled eggs, potatoes, chummus, techina, and plenty of olive oil. It's healthy and bright ... though not particularly light. This version takes the best of those Sabich flavors, then lets you choose — include the potato and toss all the components together in a salad (pictured on page 3) or stuff 'em into a wrap. It's amazing either way.

1 small eggplant, *sliced into half-moons*

½ lb Yukon Gold potatoes OR 2 wraps

4 hard-boiled eggs, *halved vertically, whites only*

2 pickles, *sliced*

ISRAELI SALAD

1 cup grape tomatoes, *halved* **OR 1 diced tomato**

½ cucumber OR ⅓ English cucumber

½ red onion, *diced*

2 Tbsp lemon juice

¼ cup fresh parsley leaves

1 tsp salt

pinch coarse black pepper

1 batch Tahini-Style Dressing *(page 232)*

calories
262 calories per serving

shani taub exchange
1 bread,
1 vegetable, 1 fat

[1]   Preheat oven to 425°F. Coat a baking sheet with nonstick cooking spray.

[2]   Place eggplant into a colander; sprinkle with salt. Let sit for 20 minutes over a bowl or in the sink. Rinse; dry on paper towels. Place eggplant on prepared baking sheet; bake for 20 minutes.

[3]   If preparing the salad version, place whole potato into a pot; cover with water. Bring to a boil; cook for 30 minutes, until tender. Let cool; slice or dice potatoes.

[4]   **Prepare the Israeli salad:** In a bowl, combine tomatoes, cucumber, onion, lemon juice, parsley, salt, and pepper.

[5]   Assemble Sabich as a wrap or salad. For a wrap, line 2 wraps with eggplant slices. Top with egg white halves, pickles, and Israeli salad; drizzle with Tahini-Style Dressing. For a salad, toss potatoes with eggplant, egg white halves, pickles, Israeli salad, and Tahini-Style Dressing.

[Try This!] Double the recipe and this is a huge, gorgeous, super-filling salad that's company-worthy (if you're entertaining, use those pretty mini tricolor potatoes instead of Yukons).

Lemony Baked Falafel
(page 146)

Cucumber, Mint, & Feta Pitas
(page 147)

The mini pitas also include Israeli Salad (page 142),
Red Cabbage Salad (page 206), and Tahini-Style Dressing (page 232).

Lemony Baked Falafel

Yields 12 falafels □ Pareve
Gluten-Free □ Low Carb

"Put just one or two falafel balls on the bottom," I'd tell the man behind the counter. "And fill the rest with salad." That's how I always ordered my falafel so that I could keep it sorta healthy. Chickpeas, even when they aren't fried, aren't low in calories, but they are nutritious and filling. Enjoy these on a falafel platter with your favorite Middle-Eastern salads or tucked inside little pitas.

½ cup fresh parsley leaves

1 garlic clove

1 red onion

1 can chickpeas, *drained, rinsed, and dried*

1 tsp cumin

1 tsp coriander

juice of 1 large lemon *(3-4 Tbsp)*

1 Tbsp cornstarch

> calories
> 36 calories per falafel ball
> or 80 calories per
> mini pita sandwich
>
> shani taub exchange
> 3 falafel balls =
> 1 bread
> (3 falafel sandwiches
> with mini pitas =
> 2 breads)

[1] Preheat oven to 425°F. Coat a baking sheet with nonstick cooking spray.

[2] In a food processor, pulse together parsley, garlic, and onion. Add chickpeas, cumin, coriander, and lemon juice. Blend to combine. If the mixture seems wet on the bottom and dry on top, that's ok.

[3] Transfer contents of food processor to a bowl; mix with a spoon to evenly distribute the moisture. Add cornstarch; mix to combine.

[4] Shape mixture into 12 patties, pressing to compact the mixture. (Note: Even though balls are the classic shape for frying, the only parts of the falafel that will brown and crisp are the surfaces touching the baking sheet. That's why I shape the mixture into patties). Coat with nonstick cooking spray; bake for 20 minutes. Flip, using a thin slotted spatula; spray again, and bake an additional 20 minutes. Let cool slightly and enjoy.

[For the Family] My entire family loves falafel plates for dinner, served with lots of fresh salads and warm pita. Aside from the traditional chummus and techina, make sure there are some lighter options on your falafel plate, such as Israeli Salad (page 142), Turkish Salad (page 80), Red Cabbage Salad (page 206), and Eggplant Puree (page 130) instead of babaganoush. You can also serve a lighter alternative Techina (Tahini-Style Dressing, page 232).

Cucumber, Mint, & Feta Pitas

Yields 4 servings   ▫   Dairy

The salad in these pitas is one that I prepare often for company. When serving as a salad, I toast some pita chips to add to the bowl (you can follow the toasting instructions on page 54). For a lunch, though, it works as a refreshing and crunchy filling inside your sandwich.

1 English cucumber, *diced*

5 celery stalks, *trimmed and diced*

1 Tbsp white wine vinegar

1 tsp dried mint

¼ cup fresh mint, *chopped (optional)*

½ tsp salt, *or to taste*

2 oz light feta cheese, *shredded or crumbled*

pita bread, *for serving*

calories
30 calories per serving for salad; plus bread

shani taub exchange
Entire salad =
1 protein, 1 vegetable
2 mini pitas = 1 bread

[1]   In a large bowl, combine cucumber and celery with white wine vinegar, mint, and salt. Add feta. Taste and add salt if necessary (as feta is salty, you might not need more).

[2]   Stuff into pita if enjoying as a sandwich.

Sunday Egg White Salad Sandwich

Yields 1 serving □ Pareve
Sugar-Free

I really do like egg salad; I even like egg white salad, especially when it's as flavorful as this one. What I really don't like, though, is preparing egg salad. I don't like peeling hard-boiled eggs. The only time I do have the patience to peel is Shabbat morning, as they are a staple on the Shabbat lunch table. I always prepare extra; sometimes they're finished and sometimes there are leftovers. Saturday night is therefore the perfect time to prepare egg white salad … with most of the work already done. That's what makes this the perfect sandwich for Sunday lunch.

EGG-WHITE SALAD

6 hard-boiled egg whites, *finely diced*

1 Tbsp light mayonnaise

1 tsp Dijon mustard

1 tsp lemon juice

2 Tbsp finely diced red onion

1 celery stalk OR small kohlrabi, *finely diced*

2 tsp capers OR finely diced pickles

½-1 tsp salt, *to taste*

FOR ASSEMBLY

2 radishes, *thinly sliced* **OR 1 handful Romaine or butter lettuce**

¼ avocado, *sliced (optional)*

microgreens, *for garnish*

1-2 slices toasted whole wheat bread, 1 small wrap, OR 1 scooped-out bagel half

calories
149 calories for entire egg white salad; plus bread

shani taub exchange
1 protein, 1 fat, 1 bread
for entire sandwich

[1] In a bowl, combine egg whites, mayonnaise, mustard, lemon juice, red onion, celery, and capers. Season with ½ tsp salt. Taste; add additional ¼-½ teaspoon salt, if desired.

[2] Layer radishes, avocado (if using), egg white salad, and greens on your bread of choice. Close, roll up, or enjoy your sandwich open-faced.

[Shani Says] Don't be scared of carbs! One slice of bread is only 60 calories, yet people are afraid to eat bread. They don't realize that vegetables have calories too … a bag of broccoli is about 180 calories. Eating in proportion will make you feel light, energetic, and healthy, so never overdo it with any one food group.

I could live in this chapter. -Victoria

Dairy dishes are most women's biggest temptation and they're not usually the most filling. That's why dishes like these are a big help. You can enjoy all the foods you love and still lose weight. -Shani

Dairy

(creamy,
cheesy, &
all you really want)

Secrets
Cauliflower Cream

Yields 6 (½-cup) servings ▫ Dairy
Gluten-Free ▫ Low Carb ▫ Sugar-Free

Cauliflower cream makes a great replacement for heavy cream or cheese. I also use this cream to sneak some veggies and protein into my children's pasta dishes, such as a replacement for ricotta in baked ziti. We use it in our Eggplant Parmesan (page 160) and over Zucchini Pizza Fries (page 162).

1 *(24-oz)* **bag frozen cauliflower**
½ cup reserved cauliflower cooking water

1 *(6-oz)* **container plain Greek yogurt**
1½ tsp salt, *plus to taste*

calories
42 calories per serving

shani taub exchange
⅓ vegetable, ⅙ protein

[1] Place frozen cauliflower into a pot. Cover with water; bring to a boil. Boil for 5 minutes. Drain (reserving ½ cup cooking water).

[2] In a blender or food processor, combine cauliflower, reserved water, yogurt, and salt. Blend until smooth.

[Good to Know] How many calories do you save by using cauliflower cream? 1 cup of cauliflower cream is 84 calories. 1 cup of ricotta is over 400 calories, and 1 cup of heavy cream is almost 800 calories!

Secrets
Pizza Tricks

Add a pizza dip! When you're busy dipping your slice, it takes longer to finish your dish and adds to the enjoyment overall. The dip doesn't have to add significant calories, either. To make a personal pizza dip, simply combine 1 tablespoon light mayonnaise with 1 tablespoon marinara sauce. Add little pinches of Italian seasoning and chili, cayenne, or red pepper if you like it spicy.

Even if you're only include ½ to 1 ounce of cheese on your pizza (such as these light wrap versions), fool yourself (or others!) into thinking it's much cheesier than it actually is. Add raw egg whites on top of the sauce before baking; they'll turn white while baking, just like melted cheese. Appearances matter! You'll enjoy your pizza way more than you would have enjoyed that barely-any-cheese version.

Secrets
It's in the Sauce

45-Calorie Marinara
Yields 3 cups   ▫   Pareve

Store-bought marinara sauce is 90 calories for ½ cup! "No sugar added" varieties are a little better, at 60 calories per ½ cup. But you really don't need that extra oil or sugar for great sauce. It's super simple to make your own. I make this quick and easy 45-Calorie Marinara in big batches (that doesn't entail more work) so I always have plenty of sauce on hand.

1 *(28-oz)* **can crushed tomatoes**
1 tsp salt
4 grinds fresh black pepper
1 tsp basil
1 tsp oregano
1 tsp garlic powder
1-2 packets sweetener, *optional*

[1] Place crushed tomatoes into a saucepan over medium-low heat.

[2] Season with salt, pepper, basil, oregano, and garlic powder. Let cook for 30 minutes. The sauce will thicken and sweeten as it cooks and it will lose its acidic quality. Add sweetener, if desired, to taste.

calories
45 calories per
½ cup serving

Gourmet Chunky Marinara

Yields 4 cups ▫ Pareve

When you have a great, flavorful sauce in the fridge, you don't need much else to complete a dish. I'll throw this on top of whatever roasted veggies I have on hand and add some cheese (and cauliflower cream for extra creaminess!) and I'm set. Use it wherever you'd use sauce, to up the gourmet factor without upping the calories.

1 red pepper

6 tomatoes on the vine
(Roma tomatoes), halved

1 onion, *sliced*

3-4 garlic cloves

1½-2 tsp salt, *or to taste*

4 grinds coarse black pepper

1 tsp dried basil

pinch smoked paprika, *or to taste*

calories
47 calories per cup

[1] Heat a stove grate over medium-high heat. Place red pepper on the grate. Roast pepper, turning every few minutes, until blistered on all sides. Let cool; peel pepper and discard peel. Remove and discard stem and seeds.

[2] Meanwhile, preheat broiler. Line a baking sheet with aluminum foil; coat with nonstick cooking spray. Add tomatoes (cut side down), onion, and garlic. Spray with nonstick cooking spray; toss to coat. Broil until tomatoes and onions are blistered, 8-10 minutes. Remove tomatoes from baking sheet; peel off and discard blistered skin.

[3] In a blender, combine red pepper, onion, and garlic. Blend until smooth. Add tomatoes; pulse a few times until they break down a bit (since tomatoes are the star, I want to see chunks of tomatoes while hiding the other ingredients). Season with salt, pepper, basil, and smoked paprika.

[Shani Says] Commercial sauces that are this low in calories don't exist ... and there are so many ways to enjoy a good sauce, including over chicken and fish.

Secrets
Alt-Pastas

Pasta substitutions save loads of calories while still giving that fork-twirling satisfaction. Here are our favorite noodle subs.

Spaghetti Squash

To cook a spaghetti squash without having to slice through the hard winter squash peel, simply throw your squash into the oven or micro-wave (no need to pierce it first). Roast at 400°F or heat until it's soft and lightly golden on all sides (usually 40 minutes to 1 hour in the oven, depending on the size; or about 12 minutes in the microwave), then cut in half, scrape out the seeds, salt the strands, and use them in your desired dish. If your squash is very large and you find that parts are still raw after opening, simply return that section to the oven or microwave. Spaghetti squash is perfect when paired with our Skinny Alfredo sauce (page 167).

Shirataki Noodles

Shirataki noodles are made from the "calorie-free" Japanese yam (although the final product does contain negligible calories, about 15, per serving). They're sold in bags in the refrigerated section of mainstream supermarkets. You'll find them next to the tofu and other vegetarian products. And while they might not look appealing in their bag, they actually work well in the right recipe. We love them best in the Shirataki Lo Mein (page 128). You can also pair them with our Butternut Squash Cream Sauce (page 166). To prepare the noodles, first rinse well in a colander, then "dry-fry," by sautéing for a couple of minutes (no oil or cooking spray necessary), and use as directed in the recipe.

Julienned Zucchini

You don't need a spiralizer to prepare zucchini noodles, also popularly known as "zoodles." A simple julienne peeler (which looks like a traditional peeler with added teeth) will do. After julienning, you can "cook" your noodles either in the microwave (as we do when preparing the Zucchini Parmesan Pasta, page 168, for a quick lunch) or give them a quick sauté in a pan.

Eggplant Parmesan

Yields 6 servings as a side (double the portion for a main dish) □ Dairy
Gluten-Free □ Low Carb □ Sugar-Free

I'd take this over a traditional eggplant parm any day. I can honestly say that I don't feel I'm missing out. I especially love telling people that they can even eat the entire 9- x 13-inch pan for dinner and still be within a normal calorie count (though I'm sure you'll be full before you get halfway through).

1 large *(1¼-lb)* **eggplant,** *sliced into rounds*

salt, *for sprinkling*

1 cup marinara sauce (pages 156-157)

1 cup cauliflower cream *(page 153)*

1¾ oz shredded mozzarella cheese, *divided*

calories
81 calories per serving

shani taub exchange
⅓ vegetable, ⅓ protein

[1]   Preheat oven to 400°F.

[2]   Place eggplant rounds into a colander; sprinkle with salt. Let sit 20-30 minutes over a bowl or in the sink; rinse and pat dry.

[3]   Coat a parchment paper-lined baking sheet with nonstick cooking spray. Add eggplant slices; coat with nonstick cooking spray. Bake for 20 minutes.

[4]   Lay half the eggplant slices in a single layer in a 9- x 13-inch baking dish. Top with ½ cup marinara sauce and ½ cup cauliflower cream. Use a spoon or spatula to spread the sauces evenly over the eggplant. Sprinkle with ¾ ounce mozzarella.

[5]   Add a second layer of eggplant, marinara, and cauliflower cream. Sprinkle with remaining 1 ounce mozzarella. Bake, uncovered, for 40 minutes.

[For the Family] Serve this to the whole family or even to company! No one will know it's lighter than usual. I much prefer, though, to save the extra portions for myself and enjoy them for lunch later in the week.

[Make Ahead] Make a triple recipe and keep extra batches in the freezer (this way you'll use up your entire batch of cauliflower cream).

[Shani Says] Simply use a bit less cheese — 1½ ounces — and you can count this ENTIRE recipe as 2 proteins and just 1 vegetable. Enjoy it!

Zucchini Pizza Fries

Yields 2 servings   □   Dairy

I don't think these ever made it off the tray before being finished. Who misses French fries?

2 zucchinis, *halved, then cut into wedge-like fries*

1 tsp salt

½ cup marinara sauce *(pages 156-157)*

½ cup cauliflower cream *(page 153)*

1 oz shredded cheese

calories
111 calories per serving

shani taub exchange
1 protein, 1 vegetable
for entire recipe

[1] Preheat oven to 425°F. Line a baking sheet with foil; coat with nonstick cooking spray.

[2] Spread zucchini wedges in a single layer on prepared baking sheet. Season with salt; coat lightly with nonstick cooking spray. Bake for 20 minutes.

[3] Spoon marinara sauce and cauliflower cream over wedges. Sprinkle with cheese. Bake an additional 10 minutes, until cheese is melted and bubbly.

[Shani Says] For 1 bread additional, you can even bread these and enjoy instead of mozzarella sticks. Dredge the zucchini in lightly beaten egg white and coat in ⅓ cup bread crumbs (you won't be able to coat the entire batch). Continue with Step 2.

Super Creamy No-Carb "Mac" and Cheese

Yields 4 servings □ Dairy
Gluten-Free □ Low Carb □ Sugar-Free

On nights when I need to be out late and haven't eaten dinner (yes, after those live cooking shows, where everyone ends up eating but me), I love coming home, simply emptying a bag of frozen cauliflower into a bowl, and microwaving it with some salt and shredded mozzarella. It's simple, hot, wholesome, and comforting. This takes it a step further, turning cauliflower into a crazy creamy dreamy mac-and-cheese. My children tasted one bite and said, "Mom, you can't have any. We're finishing it." Yes, though it does contain butter and whole milk in very tiny quantities, just a bit of them makes this taste way richer than it is. Substitutions won't work.

1 Tbsp whipped butter OR 2 tsp stick butter

1 Tbsp flour *(or gluten-free thickener of your choice)*

1½ cups whole milk

3 tsp salt, *divided*

2 *(24-oz)* **bags frozen cauliflower florets,** *completely thawed and drained*

2½ oz *(½ cup PLUS 2 Tbsp)* **shredded mozzarella AND/OR cheddar cheese,** *divided*

calories
210 calories per serving

shani taub exchange
1 protein,
1 vegetable, ¾ fat
per serving

[1]   Preheat oven to 350°F. Melt butter in a small saucepan. Whisk in flour. Add milk; whisk to combine. Bring to a slow boil over medium-high heat; cook until sauce is very thick and not watery (be careful not to burn!). It should coat the back of a spoon. Season sauce with 1 teaspoon salt.

[2]   Add thawed cauliflower to a colander and press to get out as much water as possible. In a large bowl, toss cauliflower with remaining salt, sauce, and about 1½ ounces of cheese. Transfer to 9- x 13-inch baking dish. Sprinkle remaining cheese on top. Bake for 45-60 minutes.

[Good to Know] It's super important to thaw and drain your cauliflower — squeeze out that water! You don't want the cauliflower to release liquid while baking and dilute the creaminess of the dish.

[For the Family] I hope your kids let you have at least some of this.

I wrote the dairy chapter of this book way before I teamed up with Shani, because that's the kind of food I love on a daily basis. These are a couple of my regular dishes I'd quickly whip up whenever I was serving my kids pasta for dinner (I keep mashed butternut squash on hand in the fridge; the Skinny Pasta Alfredo, alternatively, can be made in moments with no advance prep). They're filling and so creamy, and I feel as if they're indulgent ... even though they're totally light! These yield big portions, which can be an entire meal on its own. Split into two portions if you'll be enjoying one of these as a side dish next to a piece of fish.

Butternut Squash Cream Sauce over Noodles

Yields 2 servings ◻ Dairy
Gluten-Free ◻ Low Carb ◻ Sugar-Free

¾ cup cooked mashed butternut squash
3 Tbsp low-fat milk
1 tsp salt, *or to taste, divided*

8 oz shirataki noodles OR
3 cups prepared spaghetti squash
(page 158)
¾ ounce shredded mozzarella cheese

calories
82 calories per serving

shani taub exchange
1 serving =
½ protein, ½ bread
(butternut squash has
more carbohydrates than
other vegetables)

[1] In a blender, combine butternut squash, milk, and ½ teaspoon salt; blend until smooth (this cannot be done by hand).

[2] Heat a sauté pan over medium-high heat; coat with nonstick cooking spray. Add noodles, season with remaining salt, and sauté for 1 minute. Add butternut squash mixture and mozzarella cheese; stir until cheese is melted.

[Make Ahead] Butternut squash puree freezes beautifully. Blend and freeze portions of this sauce and pull them out when you're ready to enjoy (defrost quickly in the microwave).

Skinny Pasta Alfredo

Yields 2 servings   ▫   Dairy

1 tsp butter
1 garlic clove, *crushed*
1 tsp flour
½ cup milk

1 *(6-oz)* **container plain Greek yogurt**
¼ cup Parmesan cheese
3 cups cooked spaghetti squash
(page 158)

calories
185 calories per serving

shani taub exchange
1¼ protein,
1 vegetable, ½ fat
per serving

[1] In a small saucepan, melt butter over low heat. Add garlic; cook until golden, about 1 minute. Add flour; whisk until smooth. Add milk. Continue to whisk over low heat until thickened.

[2] Whisk in Greek yogurt and Parmesan cheese; cook just until warmed through (do not overcook or bring to a boil or the sauce will get clumpy). Serve over spaghetti squash or pasta replacement of your choice (pages 158-159).

[Shani Says] A cup of spaghetti is 220 calories. Compare that to a cup of spaghetti squash at 42 calories. Spaghetti squash is also a very filling vegetable as it's made up mostly of carbs.

Zucchini-Parmesan Pasta

Yields 1 serving ▫ Dairy

Parmesan cheese will give the zucchini the cheesiest flavor while still keeping the calories low (a table-spoon of some brands is only 20 calories) and turns the zucchini from a plain vegetable side to a satiating main dish for lunch. Go ahead, double the recipe and have a huge bowl of Zucchini Parmesan Pasta! I pre-pare this one often because it's a dish that's ready in 5 minutes.

2 zucchinis, *julienned*

½ tsp salt, *or to taste*

1 tsp dried basil OR
2 tsp fresh minced basil

1 tsp minced onion/garlic OR
1 tsp fresh minced garlic

2 Tbsp grated Parmesan cheese

calories
91 calories

shani taub exchange
1 protein, 1 vegetable

[1] In a medium bowl, combine zucchini, salt, basil, minced onion, and Parmesan cheese.

[2] Microwave for 3 minutes.

[Try This!] I use a simple julienne peeler to julienne the zucchini, but a spiralizer can also be used. If you want to disguise the zucchini, peel it first. You can also add julienned yellow squash and/or caramelized onions to add another color and/or texture.

[Shani Says] Zucchini is one of the most watery and lowest calorie vegetables. The high water content also makes it filling (you might weigh more after eating lots of it, but don't worry, that's only temporary).

Red Pepper Fettuccine

Yields 2 servings □ Dairy
Sugar-Free

This dish is for those who need their hearty pasta dish. There's half a serving of pasta in each portion; eggplant stands in for the rest. It's become one of my family's all-time favorite pasta dishes, high cal or low cal. (Who needs penne alla vodka anymore? I'd rather have this!)

2 oz fettuccine or any wide, flat pasta *(such as pappardelle)*

1 eggplant, *peeled, sliced thinly lengthwise*

salt, *for sprinkling*

1-2 Tbsp Parmesan shavings, *for serving*

RED PEPPER SAUCE

1 red onion, *diced*

1 garlic clove, *crushed*

salt, *for sprinkling*

1 Tbsp tomato paste

1 red pepper, *halved, stem and seeds removed*

⅓ cup plain Greek yogurt

> calories
> 241 calories per serving
>
> shani taub exchange
> 1 bread, ½ protein,
> ½ vegetable
> (medium portion)

[1] Preheat oven to 425°F. Prepare pasta according to package instructions; set aside.

[2] Cut eggplant slices into long, thin strips a little wider than your pasta. Place into a colander; sprinkle with salt. Let sit for 20 minutes over a bowl or in the sink; rinse and dry.

[3] Place pepper cut side down on a baking sheet coated with nonstick cooking spray; bake until skin blisters, about 40 minutes. Let cool; peel pepper and discard peel.

[4] Meanwhile, add eggplant slices to a baking sheet; bake for 20 minutes.

[5] **Prepare the sauce:** Coat a sauté pan with nonstick cooking spray; heat over low heat. Add onion and garlic; sprinkle with salt. Cover pan; cook until onion is soft, 7 minutes. Stir in tomato paste.

[6] In a blender, combine onion mixture, red pepper, and yogurt.

[7] When ready to serve, coat the sauté pan with nonstick cooking spray; heat over low heat. Add pasta and eggplant strips to the pan. Add red pepper sauce; toss to coat. Season with salt to taste. Serve topped with a sprinkle of Parmesan shavings per serving.

[Shani Says] I love when vegetables are added to stretch a dish. Since a man can have 2 breads for dinner, he can have the entire recipe for only 2 breads, 1 vegetable, and ¾ protein! It's a huge dinner! Omit the Parmesan and enjoy it along with a piece of fish.

62-Gram Pizza

Yields 8 personal pizzas ◻ Dairy

Pizza isn't bad. Shani tells me she allows her clients to enjoy one slice per week. When it comes to pizza, it's just a matter of how much. A 62-gram piece of dough makes a perfect 100-calorie personal pizza dough ... just roll thinly to achieve a nice-sized pie! Though you can top simply with sauce and cheese (see the egg white trick on page 155), I like to extend the pizza-savoring moments by loading it with veggie toppings, or making a Salad Pizza for lunch, as shown on page 174.

DOUGH

¾ cup warm water	**2 cups flour**
1⅛ tsp dry yeast	**1¼ tsp salt**
pinch sugar	

FOR ASSEMBLY PER PIZZA

¼ cup marinara sauce of your choice *(page 156-157)*	**½ oz shredded cheese**
	fresh basil OR spinach leaves

calories
100 calories per dough;
167 calories with toppings

shani taub exchange
One pizza =
1 bread, ½ protein

[1] In a bowl, dissolve yeast and sugar in warm water. Add flour, then salt. Knead until a dough forms. Let rise at least 20 minutes.

[2] Preheat oven to 450°F. Line 2 baking sheets with parchment paper.

[3] Divide dough into 8 balls. Flatten balls first with your palm and fingers. Using a rolling pin on a parchment paper-lined surface, roll each ball as thinly as possible, to about a 6-inch circle.

[4] Transfer dough rounds to prepared baking sheets. Top with sauce and cheese (or desired toppings; leave dough plain if using it for Salad Pizza on page 174). Bake 6-9 minutes, to desired crispness (bake without toppings if preparing Salad Pizzas). Add fresh basil or desired dried or fresh herbs before serving.

[Good to Know] You can definitely also use store-bought dough to make single-portion pizzas; divide your 1-pound piece of dough into 8 balls (this recipe yields slightly more than 1 pound).

[Make Ahead] Parbake the doughs for 4 minutes and freeze for quick pizza anytime.

[Shani Says] Make sure to add vegetables to load up your pizza and make it more filling.

Salad Pizza

Yields 4 servings ▫ Dairy

Sure, you can enjoy this salad on its own. But a salad pizza is just more fun. Likewise, any salad works with pizza, such as the Super Light Caesar (page 52). Adding the pizza crust also makes your salad a more filling and well-rounded lunch. Keep 62-Gram Pizza crusts ready in the freezer for quick meals or side dishes like this!

4 completely baked 62-gram pizza crusts *(previous page)*

SALAD

4 oz arugula

2 tomatoes on the vine
(Roma tomatoes), *diced*

1 red pepper, *diced*

¼ red onion, *finely diced*

**1 Tbsp Parmesan cheese OR
1 oz shredded light feta cheese,**
for sprinkling

HERB BALSAMIC VINAIGRETTE

4 tsp chopped fresh basil
(4 frozen cubes)

2 Tbsp balsamic vinegar

1 Tbsp red wine vinegar

1 Tbsp water

½ tsp salt

pinch black pepper

½ tsp Dijon mustard

**1 packet Splenda or
sweetener of your choice**

2 garlic cloves, *crushed*

½ Tbsp olive oil

calories
156 calories per serving

shani taub exchange
1 bread, ½ vegetable

[1] In a large bowl, combine arugula, tomatoes, red pepper, and red onion.

[2] **Prepare the vinaigrette:** In a small bowl, whisk together basil, vinegars, and water. Whisk in salt, pepper, mustard, sweetener, and garlic. Lastly, whisk in olive oil.

[3] Add vinaigrette to salad; toss to combine.

[4] Place pizza crusts on individual plates. Use a pizza slicer to divide into four wedges. Top with salad; sprinkle with Parmesan or feta.

[Shani Says] Have one Salad Pizza for lunch
and enjoy extra salad on the side.

Ruth's Gluten-Free Pizza

Yields 12 medium pizzas ▫ Dairy
Gluten-Free ▫ Low Carb ▫ Sugar-Free

The best vegetable-based pizza crust I ever tasted was made by Ruth Bendkowski, a talented personal chef who is especially adept and creative when creating dishes for those who have food intolerances. I didn't need the crust to taste like it was flour-based, but it did have to deliver a great flavor on its own (crispy edges: essential!).

CRUST

1 *(24-oz)* **bag frozen cauliflower,** *slightly thawed*

4 egg whites

2 oz *(½ cup)* **shredded mozzarella cheese**

½ cup grated Parmesan cheese

1 tsp dried basil OR oregano

1 tsp garlic powder

½ tsp salt

pinch coarse black pepper

calories
57 calories per pizza

shani taub exchange
2 pizzas = 1 protein

TOPPING

12 Tbsp marinara sauce

12 sun-dried tomatoes, *halved*

4 Tbsp grated Parmesan cheese

fresh basil leaves

[1] Preheat oven to 425°F. Line 2 baking sheets with parchment paper.

[2] Add cauliflower to a food processor. Pulse until cauliflower breaks down into small grain-like bits (do not over-process). You should have 4 cups cauliflower rice. Remove to a microwave-safe bowl; microwave for 4 minutes, or sauté in a sauté pan for 4-5 minutes, until cauliflower is cooked. Remove cauliflower to a paper towel-lined colander and press to remove as much liquid as possible.

[3] In a large bowl, whisk together egg whites, cheeses, basil, garlic powder, salt, and pepper. Add cauliflower; mix well to combine.

[4] Scoop ¼-cup mounds of cauliflower batter onto prepared baking sheets, keeping each mound well-spaced (you should be able to fit 6 on one sheet). Press down to flatten. Bake for 20 minutes, until edges are golden.

[5] Top each pizza with 1 tablespoon sauce and 2 sun-dried tomato halves. Sprinkle each with 1 teaspoon Parmesan cheese. Bake for 7 minutes, until cheese is melted; top with basil.

[Make Ahead] These crusts freeze well. Bake completely (don't overbake), then layer with parchment paper and store in a ziplock bag. When ready to enjoy, add sauce and toppings; bake until warmed through.

Phyllo Pie

Yields 12 servings ▫ Dairy

This quiche-like pie is based on the traditional Syrian Spanech Jiben, the spinach quiche that's enjoyed at almost every complete dairy meal in Syrian-Jewish homes. Sure, you can prepare it without the crust top. Phyllo, though, is so thin and light; when used here it puffs up and turns beautifully golden, making this light dish both enticing and company-worthy.

1 large or 2 medium onions, *diced*

1¼ tsp salt, *plus more for sprinkling*

3 lb *(48 oz)* **frozen spinach,** *completely thawed*

1 *(16-oz)* **container low-fat cottage cheese**

4 egg whites

4 oz shredded mozzarella cheese

2½ *(12- x 17-inch)* **sheets phyllo dough**

1 tsp sesame seeds, *for garnish*

calories
74 calories per serving

shani taub exchange
1½ servings =
1 protein, ½ vegetable
(omitting phyllo)

[1] Heat a sauté pan over medium-high heat. Coat with nonstick cooking spray; add onion and lower heat. Sprinkle onion with salt. Cover pan; cook until onion is golden and caramelized, about 20 minutes, stirring occasionally. Drain any extra liquid from the pan.

[2] Meanwhile, place spinach in a colander. Press with a paper towel to drain completely.

[3] Preheat oven to 350°F.

[4] In a bowl, combine spinach, onions, and salt. Add cottage cheese, egg whites, and mozzarella cheese. Pour into a 9- x 13-inch baking pan or oven-to-table dish.

[5] Cut whole phyllo dough sheets in half (you need 5 half-sheets). Place phyllo sheets over spinach, tucking in sheets at each edge, and coating each sheet with nonstick cooking spray before adding next sheet. Sprinkle with sesame seeds. Bake for 60-70 minutes, until spinach is set.

[Good to Know] This spinach mixture makes the perfect satisfying creamed spinach dish. There's no need to bake. After combining all the ingredients, simply sauté or microwave your portion until the egg whites are cooked through.

[Shani Says] Divide the spinach mixture into 8 individual pans. You can freeze it raw or baked. This way, you can pull out portions to warm and enjoy along with a salad for lunch. Enjoying for dinner? Most women can have 2 of these portions (¼ of the whole recipe!) along with a salad and still have a bread/grain too!

Jumbo Broccoli Baked Potatoes

Yields 6 as a main; 12 as a side   □   Dairy
Gluten-Free

Potatoes might have a bad rap, but they're one of the most diet-friendly foods you can eat, if prepared correctly. Baked potatoes rank #2 on the Satiety Index, which means they do an amazing job of satisfying hunger. And while traditional stuffed baked potatoes are loaded with butter and sour cream and lots of calories, these achieve all that fluffiness and creaminess at a low calorie count.

6 *(6-oz)* **Idaho potatoes**
1 *(24-oz)* **bag chopped frozen broccoli,** *thawed*
2 tsp salt, *divided*

1 *(5.3- or 6-oz)* **container plain Greek yogurt**
¼ cup low-fat milk
1½ oz shredded mozzarella cheese

calories
200 calories per
whole potato (2 halves)

shani taub exchange
1 bread, ½ protein,
¼ vegetable
per potato

[1] Preheat oven to 400°F. Place potatoes onto a baking sheet or in a baking pan. Coat with nonstick cooking spray; bake for 1 hour. Let cool.

[2] Meanwhile, line a baking sheet with foil; coat with nonstick cooking spray. Toss broccoli with 1 teaspoon salt; spread in a single layer on prepared baking sheet. Bake for 20 minutes.

[3] When potatoes are cool enough to handle, slice in half and scoop out the flesh, leaving a thin layer. Return potatoes skins to the oven for 10 minutes to crisp.

[4] Using a fork, mash potato flesh until smooth. Add yogurt, milk, remaining 1 teaspoon salt, and roasted broccoli; mix to combine. Return mixture to potato skins; top with cheese. Return to oven until cheese is melted and golden on top, about 15 minutes. You can broil the potatoes at this point if you like them really brown and crispy.

[Good to Know] The most important part in the preparation of these potatoes is to mash the potato flesh until completely smooth before incorporating the yogurt and milk.

[For the Family] All my kids love these potatoes; they're a staple on the dinner rotation, and I'm thrilled they enjoy something filling and nutritious.

[Shani Says] Pair this with a tilapia fillet and enjoy a filling meal!

Portobello Mushroom Towers

Yields 2 large servings □ Dairy
Gluten-Free □ Low Carb □ Sugar-Free

One summer Sunday afternoon, my family and I passed through Monsey, stopping at the Evergreen shopping center. I really wanted iced coffee, so I headed to Hava Java. As I waited for my Skinny Frappe (one of the best ever), I watched the hot dishes emerge fast from the kitchen. One dish that caught my attention was the towering Portobello Mushroom Sliders. I went home and recreated the dish ... and it was just as good as it looked.

MUSHROOMS

2 **Portobello mushroom caps**
¼ **cup red wine vinegar**
½ **tsp garlic powder**
½ **tsp dried basil**
½ **tsp salt**

TOPPINGS

1 **red pepper**
½ **onion,** *sliced*
1 **tsp salt,** *plus more for sprinkling*
½ **onion,** *diced*
8 **oz frozen spinach,** *thawed, drained*
2 *(1-oz)* **slices Muenster OR mozzarella cheese**

calories
181 calories per serving

shani taub exchange
1 protein, 1 vegetable

[1] Place mushroom caps into a ziplock bag. Add red wine vinegar, garlic powder, basil, and salt. Seal; marinate for 1 hour or up to overnight in the refrigerator.

[2] Preheat oven to 400°F. Place mushrooms and marinade into a baking pan; bake for 25 minutes.

[3] Meanwhile, place red pepper into the oven (on its own or in a baking pan). Roast until skin is blistered, about 35-45 minutes. Let cool; peel and discard peel and seeds. Slice pepper; set aside.

[4] Coat a sauté pan with nonstick cooking spray; heat over medium-high heat. Add sliced onion; lower heat and sprinkle with salt. Cover; cook, stirring occasionally, until onions are golden, about 15 minutes. Remove from pan; set aside.

[5] Coat the sauté pan again with nonstick cooking spray; heat over medium-high heat. Add diced onion; lower heat and sprinkle with salt. Cover; cook, stirring occasionally, until onions are soft, about 5 minutes. Add spinach; cook an additional 2 minutes. Season with salt.

[6] **Assemble the towers:** Top each mushroom with half the spinach mixture, half the peppers, and half the onions. Top with one slice of cheese; bake until cheese is golden and bubbling, 9-10 minutes.

[Make Ahead] All the components of this dish can be made ahead and stored separately in the refrigerator for up to 1 week. Simply assemble and bake when ready to enjoy.

Chicken & Meat

(make mains exciting again)

"Chicken again? ... Chicken again?"
Chicken is likely the most popular
go-to protein; it's healthy, lean, and
very filling. It has the same calories
and nutrients as fish, but because it's
more substantial than fish, for many
it's more satisfying. -Shani

Secrets
Take It for Lunch

You can transform the leftovers of most of these dishes into a new flavorful lunch simply by mixing and matching components you have in your fridge. Here's what you'll need to pull out to make a great wrap or sandwich to fill you up at midday. Be creative ... there IS a lunch in there.

→ Something creamy. Even just a bit adds flavor to every bite. We had the Pesto Mayo leftover from our Caramelized Onion & Salmon Wraps (page 234). Any dressing will work as long as it's not too watery.

→ Choose your protein. Grilled or pulled chicken, turkey cold cuts, egg white omelettes, or canned tuna are all good picks. If your chicken is also flavored, build the rest of the sandwich along the same flavor profile; e.g., do you have leftover Salsa Chicken (page 190)? Keep the other components also Mexican-inspired.

→ Crunch! Sandwiches need that fresh component. Romaine lettuce and cabbage are both great picks.

→ Add a flavor bonus. Sautéed onions, pickles, fresh herbs or micro-greens, sliced tomatoes, olives, avocado, roasted peppers ... what else can you add in that'll complement the other flavors?

12-Clove Kabobs

12 (2-ounce) skewers □ Meat
Gluten-Free □ Low Carb □ Sugar-Free □ Whole30 □ Paleo

I've often been asked, "How do you keep grilled chicken from getting dry?" My first piece of advice always is: Use skinless, boneless chicken thighs when grilling. Baby chicken is a can't-miss — no oil necessary. And though it has a few more calories than chicken breast, it makes up for it because we don't need to add much for it to taste great. Bonus: Diet or no diet, this is one the whole family loves.

1½ lb skinless, boneless chicken thighs (baby chicken), **cut into chunks**
¼ cup lemon juice
12 garlic cloves, *crushed*

1 tsp dried oregano
½ tsp dried basil
1 tsp kosher salt
2 lemons, *sliced, optional*

calories
72 calories per skewer

shani taub exchange
1 protein per skewer

[1]   In a bowl, combine chicken, lemon juice, garlic, oregano, basil, and salt. Cover; marinate for at least 2 hours or up to overnight in the refrigerator.

[2]   Coat a grill or grill pan with nonstick cooking spray. Heat over medium-high heat.

[3]   Meanwhile, add chicken to skewers. Optionally, you can alternate chicken pieces with lemon slices, as shown. Add to grill (you should hear a sizzle); cook for about 4-5 minutes per side.

Salsa Chicken

Yields 4 servings □ Meat

Gluten-Free □ Low Carb □ Sugar-Free □ Whole30 □ Paleo

Everyone, myself included, needs those kinds of dishes in their repertoire — dishes that they can pull out of their back pocket in thirty seconds when there really isn't time to cook. This is one such dish. Salsa is such a magical condiment (too bad we're always enjoying it with fried tortilla chips) … it has so much flavor for so few calories! Make sure to keep a couple of jars of really good-quality salsa that you love in your pantry for times like this. This concept also works using your slow cooker. Simply season your chicken, throw it in with the salsa, and go.

1½ lb skinless, boneless chicken breasts or thighs

salt, *for sprinkling*

black pepper, *for sprinkling*

4 garlic cloves, *crushed*

1 *(approximately 15.5-oz)* **jar favorite salsa**

calories
221 calories per serving

shani taub exchange
2 proteins per serving

TACO SPICE MIX

1 Tbsp chili powder

½ tsp smoked paprika

½ tsp garlic powder

½ tsp onion powder

½ tsp cumin

½ tsp oregano

[1]   Preheat oven to 350°F.

[2]   **Prepare the taco spice mix:** In a small bowl, combine chili powder, smoked paprika, garlic powder, onion powder, cumin, and oregano.

[3]   Place chicken into a baking pan. Sprinkle with salt and pepper; rub with garlic. Sprinkle chicken liberally with spice mix.

[4]   Spread salsa over chicken. Bake for 25 minutes.

[Good to Know] This dish is even better when prepared ahead and left to marinate.

[Shani Says] You can also cook fish with salsa. I also recommend enjoying it as a Shabbos dip with your matzah.

Chicken Marsala

Yields 4 servings ▫ Meat

Gluten-Free (use alternative flour) ▫ Low Carb ▫ Sugar-Free ▫ Paleo (use alternative flour)

In everyday cooking, it's my natural inclination to make dishes as light as possible. When one reader asked me for my Chicken Marsala recipe, this is what I shared. The technique is simple; the sauce is rich and deeply flavorful without the usual margarine, and lots of mushrooms help make this a hearty main.

1¾ cups *(1 [12.7 oz] bottle)* **marsala wine**

2 cups chicken broth

1½ lb thinly sliced skinless, boneless, chicken breasts

salt, *for sprinkling*

pinch coarse black pepper

2 Tbsp flour OR cornstarch, PLUS 1 tsp, *divided*

1 Tbsp oil

16 oz baby bella mushrooms, *sliced*

1 Tbsp water OR stock, *if needed*

1 small onion, *sliced*

1 garlic clove, *crushed*

1 Tbsp tomato paste

1 tsp lemon juice

¼ tsp dried oregano

calories
308 calories per serving

shani taub exchange
2 proteins

[1] Add wine to a saucepan. Bring to a boil; cook until reduced to 1 cup, about 8 minutes (have a measuring cup handy so you can determine when it's reached 1 cup). Add chicken broth; bring to a boil. Cook until total liquid reduces by half to 1½ cups.

[2] Meanwhile, season chicken with salt and pepper. Place 1 tablespoon flour into a shallow dish. Add chicken and sprinkle with additional 1 tablespoon flour, spreading over the surface. Shake off excess.

[3] Heat a sauté pan over high heat. Coat with nonstick cooking spray; add oil, swirling pan around to coat. Add chicken; cook, about 3 minutes per side. Remove from pan; set aside.

[4] Spray pan again if necessary. Add mushrooms to the pan and cook, stirring occasionally, until deeply brown, about 8 minutes (add 1 tablespoon water or stock if needed to avoid burning). Remove from pan; set aside.

[5] Add onion to the pan; cook for 3 minutes (spray pan again if needed). Add garlic and tomato paste; cook an additional 2 minutes. Add lemon juice and oregano.

[6] Add reduced marsala-chicken broth sauce to the pan. Bring to a simmer, scraping up the bits from the bottom of the pan. Return chicken to the pan; simmer in the sauce for 3 minutes. Sprinkle with 1 teaspoon flour (or 1 teaspoon cornstarch dissolved in a bit of water) to thicken sauce.

[7] Return mushrooms to the pan in the last minute of cooking; toss to coat. Season with salt to taste.

Spinach-Stuffed Chicken Thighs

Yields 10 stuffed chicken thighs   ▫   Meat
Gluten-Free   ▫   Low Carb   ▫   Sugar-Free

One of my favorite Shabbat-worthy chicken dishes is the "Eggplant-Wrapped Chicken" from Passover Made Easy. Sure, it has loads of oil and calories, but I rationalize that it's for special occasions, not everyday meals! I knew, though, I could make a just-as-special Shabbat chicken dish that was lighter too.

2 lb skinless, boneless chicken thighs
1½ Tbsp water

1½ Tbsp olive oil
fresh baby spinach OR basil leaves, *torn, for garnish*

FILLING

½ cup sun-dried tomatoes *(not packed in oil), optional*
1 large onion, *chopped*
pinch salt
3 garlic cloves, *crushed*

2 Tbsp fresh chopped basil *(6 frozen cubes)*
5 oz fresh baby spinach
½-1 tsp salt, *to taste*

WET SPICE RUB

2 tsp garlic powder
2 tsp onion powder
2 tsp dried basil
1 tsp dried parsley
1 tsp dried thyme
1½ tsp salt

⅛ tsp black pepper
pinch crushed red pepper
¼ cup red wine vinegar
2 Tbsp Dijon mustard
2 Tbsp low-fat mayonnaise

> calories
> 145 calories
> per chicken thigh
>
> shani taub exchange
> 1½ stuffed thighs =
> 2 proteins

[1] Preheat oven to 350°F.

[2] **Prepare the filling:** If using sun-dried tomatoes, soak them in hot water for 15 minutes. Drain.

[3] Heat a sauté pan over medium-high heat; coat with nonstick cooking spray. Add onion, salt, and garlic. Lower heat; cook until onions are soft, 7 minutes. Stir in basil.

[4] In a food processor, combine tomatoes, onion mixture, and spinach. Blend to combine. Transfer to a bowl; stir in salt to taste.

[5] **Prepare the spice rub:** In a bowl, combine all spices. Stir in red wine vinegar, mustard, and mayonnaise to form a paste.

[6] In a bowl, combine chicken and half the spice rub; toss to coat. Stuff chicken with spinach mixture and place into a baking pan, seam side down. Whisk water and olive oil into reserved spice rub; pour over chicken. Top chicken with fresh spinach or basil leaves. Bake, uncovered, for 45 minutes.

Steamed Chicken
and Broccoli
(page 200)

Homemade
Chinese Takeout

Shirataki Lo Mein
(page 128)

Sesame Chicken
(page 198)

Missing your
favorite takeout?
Recreate it and enjoy this
Asian-inspired spread!

One-Pan Glazed
Green Beans
(page 88)

Sesame Chicken

Yields 3 servings □ Meat
Gluten-Free

I first realized that it was entirely possible to make light Chinese dishes that were just as enjoyable when I tried to lighten up the Eggplant Chicken in Garlic Sauce from Secret Restaurant Recipes … with great results. If it worked there, it had to work with sesame chicken too, which I consider a must-have for this book. With a minimal amount of sugar, this one is a sweet, satisfying, and family-friendly replacement for the takeout favorite.

CHICKEN

1¼ lb skinless, boneless chicken breasts, *cut into nuggets*

2 Tbsp cornstarch

1 tsp sesame seeds

chopped scallions, *for garnish*

SAUCE

4½ Tbsp soy sauce

3 Tbsp water

3 Tbsp brown sugar

1½ tsp sesame oil

2 Tbsp rice vinegar

2 garlic cloves, *crushed*

1 tsp minced fresh ginger

1 tsp cornstarch dissolved in 1 Tbsp water

> calories
> 290 calories per serving
>
> shani taub exchange
> 2 proteins, 1 fruit,
> ¼ bread

[1] In a bowl, toss chicken with cornstarch. Set aside until ready to cook.

[2] **Prepare the sauce:** In a small saucepan, combine soy sauce, water, brown sugar, sesame oil, rice vinegar, garlic, and ginger. Bring to a boil. Stir in cornstarch mixture; return to a boil until sauce thickens. Remove from heat; set aside.

[3] Heat a sauté pan over medium-high heat; coat with nonstick cooking spray. When hot, add chicken; cook until golden on all sides, about 2-3 minutes per side. Add sauce and toss, letting the sauce thicken to coat the chicken.

[4] Transfer chicken to a serving dish or plates; sprinkle with sesame seeds and scallions.

[Shani Says] This supper is a healthy treat. While I wouldn't usually recommend adding sugar to a main dish, it's important for people not to feel deprived of their favorite dishes and to be able to enjoy them in a lighter way. There is 1 fruit in the exchange because of the added sugar.

Steamed Chicken and Broccoli

Yields 2 servings □ Meat

If there's one fast food dish without a mystery quantity of calories, it's Steamed Chicken and Broccoli (or steamed chicken paired with any veggie) … and my favorite is the one prepared at Glatt Bite in Lakewood, New Jersey. Sometimes, super simple, wholesome things can be very satisfying and comforting, and that's why I love it. I mix all the rice, chicken, and broccoli together and season it simply with salt and soy sauce. To learn this technique, I visited the Glatt Bite kitchen, where I watched the cooks as they steam it to achieve the perfect tenderness. Whether you make it at home or order it to go, this is one takeout meal you can actually feel good about.

2 skinless, boneless chicken breasts
1 Tbsp cornstarch

water OR chicken stock
16 oz broccoli florets
(or vegetables of choice)

FOR SERVING

1 cup brown rice
soy sauce, *to taste*

salt, *to taste*
black pepper, *to taste*

calories
242 calories per serving;
350 calories with rice

shani taub exchange
2 proteins, 1 vegetable,
1 bread (with rice)

[1] Slice each chicken breast on a 45° angle vertically into very thin slices.

[2] Toss chicken with 1 tablespoon cornstarch. Let rest for at least 30 minutes or up to a few hours in the fridge.

[3] Heat a wok (see note below) over high heat. Coat with nonstick cooking spray (you can use a bit of oil if you like); quickly stir-fry chicken, just to cook the cornstarch exterior. Remove chicken from pan.

[4] Add 2-3 inches of water or chicken stock to wok; bring to a boil over very high heat.

[5] Once steam is rising strongly, add chicken and vegetables; cook until they fall to the bottom of the pan, about 5 minutes.

[6] Remove chicken and vegetables using a slotted spoon. Serve over brown rice; season with soy sauce, salt, and black pepper.

[Good to Know] Don't have a wok? No problem. I make this at home in a saucepan. As long as the steam is rising, the ingredients will cook well (only the ingredients on the bottom will be in liquid); just keep stirring.

Spicy Chicken Lo Mein

Yields 1 serving □ Meat

Gluten-Free □ Low Carb □ Paleo (use coconut aminos instead of soy sauce)

For a few years, as editor of Ami Magazine's Whisk, *I had designated the issue after Sukkot as "The Diet Issue." Back in 2012, I asked Leah Schapira (my co-author on both the* Made Easy *and the* Secret Restaurant Recipes *cookbook series) to go out of her comfort zone and contribute recipes to that issue. This was one of her favorites that she shared. Leah says about this chicken, "OK, I can eat this every day. I don't get tired of it. I added one teeny teaspoon of honey to the chicken, which gives it that sweet and spicy kick. For that extra 20 calories, I think it's worth it."*

6 oz chicken breast, *cut into very thin strips*

1 tsp honey

1 medium onion, *thinly sliced*

½ cup bell pepper strips *(or more if you love peppers)*

2 cups julienned zucchini AND/OR yellow squash

2 Tbsp soy sauce

calories
325 calories

shani taub exchange
2 protein, 1 veggie

LEAH'S SPICE MIX

½ tsp salt

¼ tsp paprika

pinch black pepper

¼ tsp chili powder

¼ tsp garlic powder

¼ tsp parsley flakes

[1] In a small bowl, combine all ingredients for spice mix. Rub onto damp chicken.

[2] Coat a sauté pan or wok with nonstick cooking spray; heat over medium-high heat. Add chicken; sauté until cooked through, 3-4 minutes. Add honey just before chicken is done (about 30 seconds before removing from pan); toss well. Set aside.

[3] Wipe out the pan; coat with additional cooking spray and reheat pan. Add onion; sauté over low heat until onion begins to soften, about 5 minutes. Add peppers, raise heat, and sauté an additional 2 minutes. Add squash; cook until just softened.

[4] Add soy sauce; season vegetables generously with salt and pepper. Add chicken strips; stir to combine. Taste; adjust salt and pepper if needed.

[Good to Know] You can easily double the quantity of chicken in this dish to make it a complete main dish for two people. Simply adjust the quantity of spices accordingly.

[Make Ahead] Prepare Steps 1-3 earlier in the day and complete Step 4 fresh when ready to serve.

Bistro Chicken Lettuce Wraps

Yields 6 appetizer-sized servings □ Meat

Gluten-Free □ Low Carb

Those of you who know me very well can probably guess that if I had to choose my dinner tonight, I'd probably be leafing through the dairy chapter. Despite that, if there's one chicken dish I might choose over something dairy, it's the refreshing Bistro Chicken Lettuce Wraps I've been ordering for the last 12 years when I visit China Bistro in Aventura, Florida. This is my version of the dish that I create at home. The hoisin sauce is an easy way to add a dimension of flavor and sweetness without lots of sugar. Buy a bottle; you'll use it again in the recipe on page 242.

1 large onion, *cut into chunks*

2 garlic cloves, *crushed*

8 oz baby bella mushrooms

1 red pepper, *cut into chunks*

1 *(8-oz)* **can water chestnuts**

salt, *for sprinkling*

1¼ lb ground chicken breast

3 Tbsp hoisin sauce

1 head butter or iceberg lettuce, *whole leaves*

calories
143 calories per serving

shani taub exchange
1 serving =
1 protein, ⅓ vegetable

[1] Place onion, garlic, and mushrooms into a food processor; pulse until very finely diced. Do not overprocess. Remove mixture from processor. Process pepper and water chestnuts until very finely diced.

[2] Coat a sauté pan with nonstick cooking spray; heat over medium heat. Add onion mixture. Sprinkle with salt. Cover and cook until soft, about 5 minutes.

[3] Uncover; add chicken to the same pan. Cook until chicken turns white, breaking up the ground chicken constantly with a large fork to make sure chicken doesn't clump together. Add pepper mixture and hoisin sauce; cook for 3-4 additional minutes.

[4] Spoon some chicken mixture into each lettuce leaf.

[Good to Know] This will also work well with ground beef ...
a little meat goes a long way here.

[Try This!] Make this a to-go lunch the next day by adding lettuce
and chicken into a low-cal whole wheat wrap (drain the liquid first).

Chicken Avocado Schwarma

Yields 3 servings ▫ Meat
Gluten-Free ▫ Low Carb ▫ Sugar-Free

This is one dinner I prepare often without even a thought. Though you don't need the wrap, I like to include it so I don't have to think about a side and it's a complete meal on its own.

1¼ lb thinly sliced skinless, boneless chicken breasts

½ tsp salt

pinch coarse black pepper

1 Tbsp olive oil

1 onion, *cut into thin strips*

1 red pepper, *cut into thin strips*

2 garlic cloves, *crushed*

2½ tsp schwarma spice blend
(see note on facing page)

2 Tbsp lemon juice

RED CABBAGE SALAD

10 oz shredded red cabbage

2 Tbsp vinegar

2 packets sweetener

1 tsp oil

1 tsp salt

FOR ASSEMBLY (OPTIONAL)

6 Tbsp mashed avocado or Avocado-Cucumber Cream *(page 126)*

low-calorie wraps

calories
280 calories
per serving plus wrap;
add 15 calories
per Tbsp avocado

- - - - - - - - - -

shani taub exchange
2 proteins, ⅓ vegetable;
add 1-2 breads if using,
1 fat for avocado

[1] Heat a sauté pan over medium-high heat. Season chicken with salt and pepper.

[2] Add olive oil and chicken to pan; cook, about 3 minutes per side. Remove from pan, let cool, and slice into thin strips.

[3] Add onion, red pepper, and garlic to the pan; cook until onion is soft, 5-7 minutes. Return chicken strips to pan; stir to combine. Add schwarma spice blend; stir until all ingredients are well-seasoned. Stir in lemon juice; remove from heat.

[4] **Prepare the red cabbage salad:** In a bowl, combine cabbage, vinegar, sweetener, oil, and salt.

[5] Serve chicken alongside Red Cabbage Salad and avocado or assemble wraps: Spread 2 tablespoons Avocado-Cucumber Cream across the bottom-center of each wrap. Top with ⅓ of the chicken/pepper mixture and red cabbage salad. Roll up tightly.

[Good to Know] Keeping spice blends in your spice drawer is a great time saver. If you don't have schwarma spice blend on hand, combine ½ tsp each cumin, paprika, coriander, garlic powder, salt, and ¼ tsp each allspice and turmeric. Make a bigger batch so you have it ready for next time!

[Shani Says] Did you know that the schwarma you enjoy at your local Middle Eastern restaurant is made up of chicken laced with lamb fat? That's the equivalent of it being deep-fried! Enjoy the flavors at home without the fat.

Pulled Chicken Tacos

Yields 4 servings ▫ Meat

This dinner is a fiesta. And while this super-juicy pulled chicken definitely goes a long way, this meal will also work using the Mushroom Chili (page 214), or serve all these fun toppings in the Fish Fajitas (page 238). Any meal where I put all the components in the center and let my family assemble their own mini tacos is automatically popular. And there's certainly lots of flavor to go around, too.

1½ lb skinless, boneless chicken breasts
1 cup canned crushed tomatoes
water, *to cover*
1 onion, *cut into chunks*
3 garlic cloves
1 tsp salt

pinch coarse black pepper
1 tsp chili powder
1 tsp garlic powder
1 tsp onion powder
1 tsp oregano
16-24 wonton wrappers

calories
250 calories per serving with 4 wonton cups; add toppings

shani taub exchange
6 oz chicken, 4 wontons = 2 proteins, 1 bread (toppings vary)

CHOICE OF TOPPINGS

Avocado-Cucumber Cream *(page 126)*
Corn Salsa *(page 239)*

Mexican Slaw *(page 239)*
Pico de Gallo *(page 126)*
store-bought salsa

[1]   Place chicken into a medium saucepan. Cover with crushed tomatoes and water. Add onion, garlic, salt, pepper, chili powder, garlic powder, onion powder, and oregano; stir to combine. Bring to a simmer; cook for 30 minutes.

[2]   Transfer chicken to a bowl. Use two forks to shred chicken. Meanwhile, bring pan liquid to a boil and cook until thickened to a sauce-like consistency.

[3]   Return chicken to the sauce; stir to combine.

[4]   **Prepare the wonton cups:** Preheat oven to 400°F. Turn a mini cupcake pan upside down. Place wonton wrappers over the inverted cups of the muffin pan. Coat with nonstick cooking spray (optionally, you can season the wonton cups as well with salt, garlic powder, and/or chili powder). Bake for 6-7 minutes, until crisp and golden at the edges.

[5]   Fill wonton cups with pulled chicken and desired toppings or serve components separately and let each person assemble personal tacos.

Chili Chicken

Yields 4 servings   ▫   Meat

Those of you who know me for a while are probably surprised that there's a bone-in chicken at all in this book .... I had to overcome my phobia to figure out the best way to cook that chicken for a quick weeknight dinner, keeping it moist while still delivering flavor for those who aren't eating the skin. Here's the solution: Buy your chicken with the skin on. Then, when seasoning, season under the skin. You'll need to sneak in there to rub that seasoning all around. Remove the skin after baking.

6 chicken thighs AND/OR drumsticks, *bone-in skin-on*

¾ lb cauliflower florets

¾ lb mini carrots *(not baby)*

juice of ½ lemon

SMOKY SPICE MIX

1½ tsp salt

¼ tsp black pepper

3 tsp smoked paprika

1 tsp chili powder

1 tsp cumin

½ tsp cinnamon

calories
258 calories per serving

shani taub exchange
1½ thighs =
2 proteins

[1] Preheat oven to 425°F. Coat a baking sheet with nonstick cooking spray.

[2] **Prepare the smoky spice mix:** In a small bowl, combine salt, pepper, smoked paprika, chili powder, cumin, and cinnamon.

[3] Loosen the skin from each chicken thigh (leaving it still attached), and season the chicken underneath with spices. You can add additional seasoning on the skin, as pictured.

[4] Arrange chicken on prepared baking sheet. Bake for 20 minutes.

[5] Meanwhile, toss cauliflower and carrots with remaining seasoning (make more spice mix if you don't have enough) and lemon juice. Add to baking sheet; continue to bake for an additional 20 minutes.

[Try This!] This spice mix also works well when you're grilling cutlets or boneless thighs.

Chicken in a Bag

Yields 5 servings □ Meat

A brine + a bag. This is the secret to the most tender chicken ever. For years, I purchased ready-to-bake whole chicken in a cooking bag. My family didn't know (and still doesn't know) that I didn't prepare those chickens from scratch. In the meantime, I knew I'd better figure out the technique for achieving that tenderness myself. Done!

1 *(3-lb)* **whole chicken**
1 onion, *quartered*

¼ bunch fresh parsley leaves

BRINE

12 cups water
½ cup salt
⅓ cup sugar

3 Tbsp olive oil
1 tsp garlic powder
1 tsp dried herbs
(oregano, thyme, parsley, and/or basil)

HERB SPICE MIX

8 garlic cloves, *crushed*
2 Tbsp fresh minced parsley
(or 6 frozen cubes)
1 tsp dried parsley leaves
2 tsp salt

1 tsp garlic powder
1 tsp onion powder
¼ tsp paprika
¼ tsp black pepper

calories
165 calories per serving

shani taub exchange
4 oz dark meat or 6 oz
white meat = 2 proteins

SPECIAL EQUIPMENT
1 oven bag

[1] **Do ahead — prepare the brine:** In a large container, combine water, salt, sugar, olive oil, garlic powder, and herbs. Add chicken; brine for at least 4 hours or up to overnight (no longer than 24 hours) in the refrigerator. Remove chicken from brine; rinse.

[2] Preheat oven to 350°F.

[3] **Prepare the herb spice rub:** Combine all spice rub ingredients. Loosen the skin in all areas where there is meat, sliding your fingers under it to get the seasoning mix to the actual meat (as the skin won't be eaten). You can also season the outside of the chicken with dried herbs, as pictured.

[4] Place oven bag into a roasting pan. Place chicken into bag. Add onion and parsley into chicken cavity. Seal bag, cover pan, and bake for 1 hour.

[5] When ready to serve, open bag and use gloved hands to transfer chicken to serving platter.

[Good to Know] You can use this technique with any spices or
seasoning to achieve super tenderness.

[Make Ahead] You can do all the steps for this chicken ahead
of time, and then simply bake fresh. It's also easy to rewarm
if baked earlier in the day. Keep the chicken in the bag.

[Shani Says] Note that even though the brine contains sugar,
it's later discarded and only a miniscule amount of brine is
actually absorbed by the chicken.

Mushroom Chili

Yields 4 servings ▫ Meat

Gluten-Free ▫ Low Carb ▫ Sugar-Free ▫ Whole30 ▫ Paleo

A pound of meat can be comprised of two steaks that can feed two people. A pound of ground meat, though, can also feed a family of 6 a nourishing and filling dinner ... when it's made into a chili and "beefed" up with lots and lots of mushrooms. Mushrooms take on a meaty flavor of their own and add to, rather than detract from, the heartiness of the stew. Each "serving" here is a very generous portion.

1 onion, *diced*

1 Tbsp salt, *plus more for sprinkling*

2 garlic cloves, *crushed*

16 oz baby bella mushrooms, *finely diced*

1 lb ground meat

1 *(28-oz)* **can crushed tomatoes**

1 Tbsp cumin

1 Tbsp chili powder

1 Tbsp garlic powder

1 tsp oregano

pinch cayenne pepper *(or more if you like it spicy)*

pinch smoked paprika *(or more if you like it smoky)*

pinch black pepper

calories
295 calories per serving

shani taub exchange
2 proteins, ¼ vegetable

[1] Heat a large pot over medium-high heat; coat with nonstick cooking spray. Lower heat, add onion and sprinkle with salt. Cover; cook until onion is soft, 5-7 minutes. Add garlic and mushrooms; cook until mushrooms are deeply brown, 15-20 minutes. Add meat; brown, breaking apart meat constantly until meat is no longer red and is cooked through, about 2 minutes.

[2] Add crushed tomatoes, cumin, chili powder, garlic powder, 1 tablespoon salt, oregano, cayenne pepper, smoked paprika, and pepper; stir to combine. Bring to a boil, lower heat to the lowest setting. Cover; simmer for 60-90 minutes.

[For the Family] My whole family enjoyed this chili. The kids don't notice that it was half comprised of mushrooms (they eat it in a taco shell). Just dice the mushrooms finely and no one will be the wiser. You can serve the chili in wonton shells (page 208) or toasted tortillas (page 126).

[Make Ahead] Yes! Chili is one of the most freezer-friendly foods.

[Try This!] Serve this with toppings (as pictured)! Festive chili accompaniments throughout this book include Avocado-Cucumber Cream (page 126), Corn Salsa (page 239), Mexican Slaw (page 239), Pico de Gallo (page 126), store-bought salsa, and salsa verde (made with tomatillos).

[Shani Says] Look for extra lean meat in your butcher's showcase.

Veggie, Beef, and Barley Stew

Yields 6 servings   □   Meat

This dish has saved me countless times. It's my go-to whenever I know I'm going to be out all day and won't be home in time to prepare dinner. It's so hearty, filling, rich, and thick, that you wouldn't even think that it's a low-calorie meal. This yields a big portion for each serving. If you're not serving 6 people, add only the meat that you need.

1½ lb minute steak

1 onion, *chopped*

3 garlic cloves, *crushed*

salt, *for sprinkling*

10 ounces baby bella mushrooms, *large ones halved*

2 carrots, *peeled and diced*

1 *(24-oz)* **bag frozen diced butternut squash**

¾ cup barley

10 cups beef stock

2 Tbsp fish-free Worcestershire sauce

calories
287 calories per serving

shani taub exchange
1 serving =
2 proteins, 1 bread

[1] Heat a sauté pan over high heat; coat with nonstick cooking spray. When pan is hot, add steak (you should hear a sizzle) and sear until brown, about 2 minutes per side. Remove meat from pan and place into slow cooker.

[2] Add onion and garlic to the pan; sprinkle with salt. Cover; sauté for 5 minutes. Add mushrooms and carrots; sauté for 5 minutes. Add to slow cooker over meat.

[3] Add butternut squash, barley, beef stock, and Worcestershire sauce to the slow cooker. Cover; cook on low for 6-8 hours.

[Good to Know] You can use lots of different veggies in this stew. Celery, sweet potato in lieu of butternut squash, and root vegetables such as rutabaga are other options.

[Make Ahead] Use a slow cooker liner so you can lift the stew out of the slow-cooker, store it in a container, and refrigerate or freeze it for another day. It will need additional water upon rewarming.

Shabbos Steaks

Yields 2 servings ▫ Meat

I was skeptical when Leah Schapira told me that I could bake steaks, covered in the oven, for hours. Sure, I had baked steaks before, but only after searing and only for a few minutes, so the inside cooks to a perfect medium-rare. The first time I tried this technique, I accidentally left the oven on when I meant to turn it off (for a couple of hours!). The rest of the food ... well, it was all still edible if you're a fan of all things crispy and crunchy. These steaks? They were still moist and tender. I paired them with this classic steak sauce (I love its aroma while it cooks!), which I also serve over any grilled meats.

2 *(4-oz)* **club steaks**
1 tsp Montreal steak seasoning
½ onion, *finely diced*
salt, *for sprinkling*

4 mushrooms, *quartered*
¼ cup red wine
1½ cups beef stock
1 tsp Dijon mustard

calories
287 calories per serving

shani taub exchange
2 proteins

[1] Preheat oven to 350°F. Coat a baking pan or baking sheet with nonstick cooking spray.

[2] Season steaks with steak seasoning. Place in prepared baking pan; cover tightly and bake for 1 hour.

[3] **Meanwhile, prepare the sauce:** Coat a sauté pan with nonstick cooking spray; heat over medium-high heat. Add onion, lower heat, sprinkle with salt, cover pan, and cook for 5 minutes. Uncover pan, raise heat to medium, add mushrooms and sauté for 3 minutes. Add wine; simmer to reduce for 2 minutes. Add beef stock and mustard; cook until sauce thickens. Set aside.

[4] Pour sauce over steaks. Cover and bake for an additional 1 hour. Keep steaks covered to rewarm.

[Good to Know] This technique will work with almost any type of steak and even veal chops.

[Shani Says] Want to know which cuts of meat are the leanest? Just look at them and you'll be able to tell, as fattier steaks have more white areas. Club steaks are one of the leaner steaks available.

Skirt Steak Over Asian Eggplant

Yields 2 servings □ Meat

Even though skirt steak is higher in fat than other cuts of meat, here's why I like it, even for a book like this: Skirt steak is best when it's pound, pound, pounded until thin. It's so stretchy! I find that when I buy just one (roughly 1-lb) package, it goes a long way in feeding a few people. Even these small 4-ounce portions appear larger than they really are.

½ lb skirt steak

1 eggplant, *sliced into rounds (use 2 Asian eggplants when in season)*

coarse black pepper, *for sprinkling*

MARINADE

2 Tbsp soy sauce

juice of ½ lime

1 tsp chili powder

1 tsp dried mint

2 garlic cloves, *crushed*

2 tsp minced ginger

calories
321 calories per serving

shani taub exchange
2 proteins, ½ vegetable

[1] Soak skirt steak in water for at least 30 minutes (this step is essential for removing the saltiness). Using a meat mallet (or the bottom of a pot if you don't have a mallet), pound steak thin.

[2] Preheat oven to 425°F. Coat a baking sheet with nonstick cooking spray.

[3] Meanwhile, place the eggplant into a colander. Sprinkle with salt; let sit for 20-30 minutes over a bowl or sink. Rinse and dry. Place eggplant onto prepared baking sheet; bake for 18 minutes.

[4] **Meanwhile, prepare the marinade:** Combine soy sauce, lime juice, chili powder, mint, garlic, and ginger.

[5] Toss eggplant with marinade.

[6] Coat a grill pan with nonstick cooking spray; heat over high heat. Season steak with black pepper. Cook for about 3 minutes per side.

[7] Slice steak into portions and serve over marinated eggplant.

[Shani Says] I do recommend skirt steak as it leaves many very satisfied, because it's one of the tastiest cuts of meat. That's also because it's very salty. Sodium retains water in the body, so be sure not to skip that soaking step, which will partially reduce the salt content.

Fish is my favorite protein of choice on most nights. -Shani

The quality of your fish matters! Premium fish will, very simply, taste better, no matter which recipe you use. -Victoria

Fish

(the light,
feel-good main dish)

Secrets
Plank It

One way to add flavor to fish without adding anything else (besides salt and pepper, of course) is to cook it on a cedar plank. You don't need a special recipe; just add your fish to the soaked plank and then grill it. After it's cooked, you can top the fish with any of the sauces in this chapter.

You can also cook the fish over citrus slices and top it with fresh herbs.

Bruschetta Salmon

Yields 3 servings □ Pareve

Gluten-Free □ Low Carb □ Sugar-Free □ Paleo □ Whole30

There are some ingredients that will very likely become pantry and fridge staples as you cook from this book. Frozen cauliflower is likely one of them (I buy lots when it's on sale!). Capers are another. They add so much calorie-free flavor, and if they're not yet a fridge staple, they should be.

3 *(5-oz)* **salmon fillets**
2 garlic cloves, *crushed*
½ sweet onion, *diced*
1 tsp salt, *divided,*
plus more for sprinkling
1 pint grape tomatoes, *halved*

¼ cup capers
¼ cup fresh parsley leaves
pinch red pepper flakes
¼ cup fresh basil leaves
½ tsp Dijon mustard
coarse black pepper, *for sprinkling*

> calories
> **215** calories per serving
>
> shani taub exchange
> **2** proteins

[1] Preheat oven to 400°F.

[2] Coat a sauté pan or frying pan with nonstick cooking spray; heat over high heat. Add garlic and onion; season with ½ teaspoon salt. Cover and lower heat to medium-low; cook for 5 minutes.

[3] Uncover pan. Add tomatoes, capers, parsley, and red pepper flakes. Raise heat to medium-high. Cook for 5 additional minutes, until vegetables release liquid and tomatoes begin to wilt. Stir in ½ teaspoon salt, basil, and mustard.

[4] Meanwhile, place salmon fillets into a baking pan; coat fish with nonstick cooking spray. Sprinkle with salt and pepper. Top salmon with tomato mixture; bake until fish flakes easily with a fork, about 20 minutes.

[Make Ahead] You can make the sauce ahead and keep refrigerated. Then simply pour it on your salmon and bake for a quick dinner!

[Try This!] You can also serve this tomato sauce over chicken, mixed into brown rice, or even over a thin crust pizza.

Stir-Fry Over Salmon

Yields 2 servings □ Pareve

Gluten-Free □ Low Carb □ Low Sugar □ Whole30 and Paleo diets, substitute coconut aminos for teriyaki sauce

I love when dishes appear to be much bigger than they actually are. That's what happens when we smother a piece of salmon with a stir-fry that takes over the entire plate. Instead of "That's all?" it's more like, "Wow, all this is for me?" This appeals to all who love the traditional (sugar-coated) teriyaki salmon, except that it's way more filling with way fewer calories. Don't use a thin teriyaki sauce (e.g., no Kikkoman); choose a thick sauce that has 25 calories per tablespoon or less ... it'll go farther.

2 (5-oz) **salmon fillets**

salt, *for sprinkling*

black pepper, *for sprinkling*

2 scallions, *white and some green, chopped*

STIR FRY

1 Tbsp sesame oil

1 onion, *thinly sliced*

1 garlic clove, *crushed*

1 tsp minced fresh ginger

½ **red pepper,** *very thinly sliced*

1 cup fresh broccoli florets, *thinly sliced,* **OR broccoli slaw**

2 Tbsp teriyaki sauce

½ **tsp salt,** *or to taste*

> calories
> 336 calories per serving
>
> shani taub exchange
> 2 proteins, ⅓ vegetable

[1] Preheat oven to 400°F. Sprinkle salmon fillets with salt and pepper.

[2] Heat an ovenproof sauté pan with nonstick cooking spray. When hot, add salmon, skin-side up, and sear for one minute. Turn salmon and sear on the two sides. Turn skin-side down, transfer to oven, and bake for 15 minutes.

[3] **Meanwhile, prepare the stir-fry:** Heat a wok or sauté pan over high heat until very hot. Add sesame oil, onion, garlic, and ginger; cook for 2 minutes, stirring constantly. Add red pepper and broccoli; cook for an additional 2 minutes. Stir in teriyaki sauce. Taste; add salt if needed.

[4] Pour stir-fry over salmon fillets on serving plate or individual dishes. Top with chopped scallions before serving.

[Try This!] Swap these veggies for any you have in your fridge. Just slice thinly and use equal quantities. I like to save a step by using half of the stir-fry from the Veggie Egg Rolls (page 124) for this dish so I can prep once for a complete dinner.

Pan-Seared Salmon
with Strawberry Balsamic Sauce

Yields 2 servings □ Pareve

Gluten-Free □ Low Carb □ Sugar-Free □ Whole30 □ Paleo

One of my family's favorite salmon dishes is my Pomegranate-Glazed Salmon. To prepare that dish, I simply reduce a bottle of pomegranate juice until it's a thick, syrupy glaze (I store that glaze in the fridge at all times for a last-minute gourmet dish). I know that the pomegranate sauce is filled with antioxidant goodness ... but also a very concentrated amount of natural sugar (and we like lots of sauce!).

Can I achieve that same fruity tart flavor with less sugar and fewer calories? Yes! And this version even tops the dish that inspired it.

2 *(5-oz)* **salmon fillets OR 10 oz salmon cubes**

salt, *for sprinkling*

coarse black pepper, *for sprinkling*

½ onion, *diced*

¼ cup balsamic vinegar

¾ cup frozen strawberries, *finely diced*

calories
286 calories per serving

shani taub exchange
2 proteins, ½ fruit

[1] Preheat oven to 400°F. Season salmon fillets with salt and pepper.

[2] Heat an ovenproof sauté pan coated with nonstick cooking spray. When hot, add salmon, skin-side up; sear for one minute. Turn salmon and sear the two sides. Turn skin-side down, transfer to oven, and bake for 15 minutes (salmon cubes will cook in 5-6 minutes after searing).

[3] **Prepare the sauce:** Heat a saucepan over medium-high heat. Coat with nonstick cooking spray. Lower heat; add onion and sprinkle with salt. Cover; cook until soft, 5-7 minutes. Add balsamic vinegar and strawberries. Bring to a boil. Lower heat; simmer for 8-10 minutes until thickened.

[4] Spoon sauce over salmon before serving.

[Try This!] Use this sear-then-bake technique to achieve a perfect crust on any fish (without the added oil and calories of pan-fried fish!).

[Make Ahead] Make a big batch of sauce ahead of time and keep it in the fridge for last-minute dinner emergencies!

Techina Salmon

Yields 3 servings □ Pareve

"Salmon with Techina-Lemon Sauce" was another one of my family's all-time fish favorites that I made often. Sure, like the pomegranate glaze mentioned on the previous page, the recipe was healthy but high in calories, and there was no way it was making it into this book. Like most of our favorite foods, though, I wasn't willing to give it up. I'd simply find another way to make it. And what happened? Again, I found a version we loved just as much, if not more! This Tahini-Style Dressing is so, so super useful, you'll find yourself enjoying it over and over (as on pages 98, 130, 142, 146, and 147)!

1 large sweet onion, *cut into thin strips*

½ tsp salt, *plus more for sprinkling*

3 *(5-ounce)* **salmon fillets**

pinch coarse black pepper

1 batch Israeli Salad *(page 142)*

TAHINI-STYLE DRESSING

2 Tbsp light mayonnaise

1½ tsp tahini paste

2 Tbsp lemon juice

1½ Tbsp water

1 garlic clove, *crushed*

1 tsp fresh minced parsley leaves

½ tsp salt

pinch cumin

calories
255 calories per serving

shani taub exchange
1 protein, 1 fat

[1] Preheat oven to 400°F.

[2] Coat a sauté pan with nonstick cooking spray; heat over low heat. Add onion, sprinkle with salt, and cover. Cook until onion is golden, about 15 minutes, stirring occasionally.

[3] Meanwhile, place salmon into a baking pan. Season with salt and pepper; coat with nonstick cooking spray. Bake for 10 minutes.

[4] **Meanwhile, prepare the dressing:** In a small bowl, whisk together mayonnaise, tahini paste, lemon juice, water, garlic, parsley, salt, and cumin.

[5] Top salmon with onion and Tahini-Style Dressing. Bake for an additional 10 minutes, or until fish flakes easily with a fork. Serve alongside Israeli salad.

[Shani Says] High cholesterol? Eat salmon. The omega-3s in it lower cholesterol. Omega-3s also help the body relax; I advise those who feel stressed or nervous to eat salmon. The higher-quality varieties usually contain the most of this nutrient.

Caramelized Onion & Salmon Wraps

Yields 4 wraps   ▫   Pareve

This wasn't on my original list of dishes I thought I'd include in this book, but it is one of those meals I prepare often as an easy one-dish dinner that leaves us satisfied. As I heated the sauté pan to prepare this yet once more, I realized: If we enjoy this simple refreshing dish so often, you will too.

4 *(5-oz)* **salmon fillets**
salt, *for sprinkling*
black pepper, *for sprinkling*
2 large sweet onions, *sliced*

2 tsp sugar
2 cups Creamy Light Cole Slaw *(page 78)*
4 low-calorie wraps

PESTO MAYO
2 Tbsp low-fat mayonnaise
2 Tbsp chopped fresh basil *(or 6 cubes)*

½ tsp whole grain Dijon mustard
½ Tbsp water
pinch salt

calories
313 calories per wrap

shani taub exchange
1-2 breads,
2 proteins, 1 fat

[1]   Preheat oven to 400°F. Season salmon fillets with salt and pepper.

[2]   Heat an ovenproof sauté pan coated with nonstick cooking spray. When hot, add salmon, skin-side up; sear for one minute. Turn salmon and sear the two sides. Turn skin-side down, transfer to oven, and bake for 15 minutes. Remove salmon skin.

[3]   Meanwhile, coat a sauté pan with nonstick cooking spray; heat over medium heat. Add onion; sprinkle with sugar. Lower heat to low; cook, stirring occasionally, until onions are golden and caramelized, about 20 minutes.

[4]   **Meanwhile, prepare the pesto mayo:** Combine all pesto mayo ingredients.

[5]   Spread mayo on wraps. Top each with a salmon fillet, onions, and coleslaw. Roll up, egg roll-style. Slice on the diagonal and serve.

[Good to Know] Avocado also goes well inside this wrap.

Fish Fajitas

Make this colorful, light dinner (page 238) that your whole family will enjoy. You can leave all the components on the table so that everyone can assemble their own fajitas.

Avocado-Cucumber Cream (page 126)

Mexican Slaw (page 239)

Corn Salsa
(page 239) →

Fish Fajitas

Yields 8 fajitas □ Pareve

Summer nights and refreshing fish fajitas … I really savor this dinner. I serve this recipe as a complete meal, as the salads that go into your fajitas also work as a side dish. The salads use the same ingredients, so it's easy to prep them simultaneously. To make this into an also-friendly-for-kids dinner, I also prepare some breaded fish, so there's a component that picky eaters can enjoy. You can also leave some of the corn plain for them.

1½ lb tilapia *(or flounder or sole)*
¼ cup lemon juice

Cajun spice blend *(see note below)*
½ Tbsp oil

FOR ASSEMBLY

4 low-calorie wraps, *halved (such as Flat-Out)*
Mexican Slaw *(facing page)*
Corn Salsa *(facing page)*

store-bought tomato salsa OR Pico de Gallo *(page 126), optional*
Avocado-Cucumber Cream *(page 126)*

calories
144 calories per fajita

shani taub exchange
For 2 fajitas: 1 bread, 2 protein, (add 1 fat for 2 Tbsp Avocado-Cucumber Cream)

[1] Preheat oven to 400°F.

[2] Add fish to a baking pan. Add lemon juice; marinate 10 minutes. Pat fish dry; coat in Cajun spice (amount depends on how spicy you like it). Heat an ovenproof skillet over high heat until smoking hot. Coat with nonstick cooking spray; add oil. Add fish to skillet. Sear for 1 minute, then transfer skillet to oven. Bake fish for 10-12 minutes, until fish flakes easily with a fork.

[3] **To assemble the fajitas:** Warm wraps by toasting them in a pan or in the oven, or by heating them briefly in the microwave (after wrapping them in a clean towel). Add 3 ounces fish to each wrap. Top with ¼-cup Mexican Slaw, 1 tablespoon Corn Salsa, 1 tablespoon tomato salsa (optional), and 1 tablespoon Avocado-Cucumber Cream. Serve with extra slaw on the side.

[Good to Know] To make your own Cajun spice blend so you can control the heat, combine 2½ teaspoons kosher salt, ¾ teaspoon freshly ground black pepper, 1 teaspoon garlic powder, 1 teaspoon onion powder, ½ teaspoon thyme, ½ teaspoon oregano, 1 tablespoon sweet paprika, and up to 1 teaspoon cayenne pepper (omit or use very little if you don't like it hot).

Mexican Slaw

Yields 5 cups ▫ Pareve

1 *(11-ounce)* **bag coleslaw mix**

½ **jalapeno,** *seeded and minced*

2 **Tbsp fresh chopped cilantro**
(OR 2 frozen cubes)

1 **tsp cumin**

2 **packets sweetener**

3 **Tbsp lime juice**

1 **Tbsp red wine vinegar**

1 **Tbsp olive oil**

1 **garlic clove,** *minced*

1 **tsp salt**

pinch coarse black pepper

calories
52 calories per cup

shani taub exchange
1¼ cups = ¼ fat

▫ In a large bowl, combine all slaw ingredients.

Corn Salsa

Yields 2½ cups ▫ Pareve

4 **ears of corn in the husk**
(1 [15-oz] can OK when not in season)

½ **jalapeno pepper,**
seeded and minced

½ **red onion,** *finely diced*

1 **tsp cumin**

2 **Tbsp lime juice**

1 **packet sweetener**

½ **tsp salt**

pinch coarse black pepper

calories
70 calories per ½ cup

shani taub exchange
1 bread

[1] Microwave the corn in the husk for 8 minutes. Let cool, remove husk, and slice kernels into a bowl.

[2] Add remaining salsa ingredients; mix well.

[Make Ahead] Slaws and salsas can be made a day ahead. They'll be even more flavorful after marinating.

Tuna Sliders

Yields 2 servings; 6 sliders □ Pareve
Gluten-Free □ Low Carb (without bun)

A few years ago, I asked a crowd of 150 women at a cooking show, "Who loves tuna?" No one raised her hand. That's what I expected. I asked, "Why?"

One woman answered, "Because it's dry." Again, the answer I expected.

I told them, "That's because you've never had it prepared correctly."

They then watched me season and sear my tuna steaks, leaving the beautiful square of pink in the middle. All the samples were wiped clean that day (and there was lots of tuna to go around) ... and each one of those women left that day with a revised opinion. Whether you're new to tuna or have loved it always, this is a different, fresh way to enjoy the delicacy.

¾ lb sashimi-grade tuna, *cubed*

2 small garlic cloves, *crushed*

½ Tbsp sesame oil

½ Tbsp soy sauce

½ Tbsp fresh minced ginger

½ Tbsp Dijon mustard

½ tsp Montreal steak seasoning

¼ tsp salt

2 scallions, *finely diced*

MUSHROOM TOPPING

½ onion, *thinly sliced*

salt, *for sprinkling*

8 oz baby bella mushrooms, *sliced*

2 Tbsp vegetable stock

ASIAN BURGER SAUCE

2 Tbsp low-fat mayonnaise

1 tsp lime juice

1 tsp soy sauce

2 tsp water

¼ tsp sriracha sauce

FOR ASSEMBLY

lettuce   low-calorie bread, wrap, OR buns

calories
75 calories per slider,
27 calories for toppings,
plus bread

shani taub exchange
2 proteins, 1 fat (for sauce);
¼ vegetable
(mushroom topping);
1 bread (depending on
type of bread used)

[1] **Do ahead:** Place tuna into a food processor. Pulse 4-5 times, until ground. Remove to a bowl; add garlic, sesame oil, soy sauce, ginger, mustard, steak seasoning, salt, and scallions. Mix to combine. Shape into 6 slider-size patties. Keep covered in the refrigerator (at least 1 hour) until ready to grill.

[2] **Meanwhile, prepare the topping:** Heat a sauté pan over medium-high heat; coat with nonstick cooking spray. Add onion; sprinkle in salt. Lower heat to medium-low. Add mushrooms and stock; cook, stirring occasionally, until mushrooms are soft and deep brown.

[3] **Prepare the sauce:** Whisk together mayonnaise, lime juice, soy sauce, water, and sriracha sauce.

[4] Coat a grill pan with nonstick cooking spray; heat until very hot. Add sliders. Cook for approximately 1 minute per side. You'll have nice grill marks on the outside; the inside should be rare. Do not let the tuna cook all the way through or it will dry out!

[5] **Assemble the sliders:** Layer lettuce, slider, mushroom/onion mixture, and sauce on your choice of bread.

[Try It!] These sliders are also delicious in their carb-free form. Skip the bun, use the sauce as a dip, and enjoy the mushrooms as a side dish.

[Good to Know] For a more affordable option, you can use salmon to make the sliders.

[Shani Says] Fresh tuna is one of my favorite foods!

Hoisin-Glazed Sea Bass & Mushrooms

Yields 2 servings ◻ Pareve
Gluten-Free

The kids had already eaten, and I had defrosted sea bass fillets for the adults. But the sauce that I envisioned to go along with the sea bass just didn't work out. It was the end of a long day and I didn't have the time or energy to think of a new idea or to start pulling out the ingredients for one of my tried-and-true options. I spotted the hoisin sauce in the fridge (I had last used it in the Bistro Chicken Lettuce Wraps on page 204), brushed it on the fish, and stuck the pan into the oven, hoping dinner would still be ok.
I received a "Spectacular!" I suppose everyone needs easy solutions for all kinds of days.

2 *(5-oz)* **sea bass fillets**
1 tsp salt, *divided*
coarse black pepper, *for sprinkling*
1 tsp fresh minced ginger
(or 1 frozen cube)
1 garlic clove, *crushed*

1 Tbsp PLUS 1 tsp hoisin sauce, *divided*
8 oz baby bella mushrooms, *halved*
2 Tbsp water
½ tsp garlic powder

calories
228 calories per serving

shani taub exchange
2 proteins, ¼ vegetable

[1] Preheat oven to 400°F. Place fish into a baking pan, coat with nonstick cooking spray, season with ½ teaspoon salt and pepper, and spread with ginger and garlic. Brush fish with 1 tablespoon hoisin sauce. Bake for 20-25 minutes, until fish flakes easily with a fork.

[2] Meanwhile, coat a sauté pan with nonstick cooking spray; heat over medium-high heat. Add mushrooms and 2 tablespoons water. Sauté until mushrooms are deeply brown and soft, about 3 minutes. Stir in remaining teaspoon hoisin sauce, garlic powder, and remaining ½ teaspoon salt. Serve mushrooms alongside sea bass.

[Good to Know] Hoisin sauce is Chinese condiment that offers a flavor profile different from teriyaki. At 25 calories per tablespoon (it's super thick, so a little goes a very long way), it offers lots of flavor bang for the calories.

[For the Family] Even though sea bass is expensive, it's a worthwhile treat and doesn't come out so costly when you need only one or two portions. Since there are not many other ingredients, the overall cost of the meal is still reasonable.

[Shani Says] While a serving of fatty fish is 2 ounces cooked, a serving of lean fish is 3 ounces cooked (fish does shrink as it cooks). Turbot is another option to try; it's similar to sea bass with a fat content that's closer to tilapia.

Lemon Zested Fillets en Papillote

Yields 2 servings □ Pareve
Gluten-Free □ Low Carb

Really, this dish will work with any fish at all. It'll also work with any vegetables you have in your fridge. It'll also work whether you want to serve an easy, complete weeknight meal (protein + veggies in one packet) or whether you're entertaining and need something with a wow presentation.

12 asparagus spears, *leaves and ends trimmed, halved vertically*

salt, *for sprinkling*

coarse black pepper, *for sprinkling*

2 *(5-oz)* **sea bass OR** *(7-oz)* **halibut OR tilapia fillets**

1 fresh lemon, *zested and then sliced into rounds*

1 leek, *white and light green parts only, cut into long, thin strips*

1 zucchini, *julienned*

¼ cup white wine

1 handful fresh parsley leaves

calories
222 calories per serving

shani taub exchange
2 proteins, ⅓ vegetable

[1] Preheat oven to 400°F.

[2] Cut two pieces of parchment paper large enough to fold over the fillets. On one side of each piece, place 6 asparagus spears; season them with salt and pepper. Place fish on asparagus. Season with salt, pepper, and lemon zest. Top with leek and zucchini. Season lightly with salt and pepper.

[3] Spoon white wine over fish and vegetables; top with lemon slices and fresh parsley. Bring the parchment paper over fish fillets and crimp the edges to form a packet. Slide packets onto a baking sheet; bake for 20 minutes.

[4] Serve fish in their parchment packets. Be careful when unwrapping as steam will be hot.

Herb & Dijon Crusted Turbot

Yields 2 servings ▫ Pareve

I received one of my best-ever fish lessons in the kitchens of Va Bene, the kosher dairy Italian restaurant in Manhattan. Leah Schapira and I were on one of our "restaurant recipe expeditions," and Giuseppe Lattanzi brought us into the back to show us how he prepares his mahi-mahi, using the simplest of fresh ingredients. While his recipe, featured in Everyday Secret Restaurant Recipes, is still a favorite, the lessons and fish cooking techniques I learned that day inspire this one too.

2 *(7-oz)* **turbot fillets**
salt, *for sprinkling*
coarse black pepper, *for sprinkling*
2 Tbsp fresh minced basil
(or 6 frozen cubes)

2 Tbsp fresh minced parsley
(or 6 frozen cubes)
2 tsp whole grain Dijon mustard
6 garlic cloves, *crushed*

calories
234 calories per serving

shani taub exchange
2 proteins per serving

[1]   Preheat oven to 400°F.

[2]   Sprinkle turbot with salt and pepper. In a bowl, combine basil, parsley, mustard, and garlic. Coat tops of fillets with mixture.

[3]   Coat an ovenproof skillet with nonstick cooking spray; heat over high heat. Add fillets, skin side down (you should hear a sizzle); cook for 2 minutes. Transfer fish to oven; bake for 20 minutes.

Janel's Moroccan-Style Fish

Yields 6 servings   □   Pareve

Gluten-Free   □   Low Carb   □   Sugar Free   □   Whole30   □   Paleo

When my sister-in-law first learned about this cookbook, she said this is the fish I have to include. "It's light, filling, guilt-free ... and cookbook-worthy!" she said.

"There's no way you make this whole recipe," I told her when she gave me the instructions, "You and Joey aren't finishing two pounds of fish!" (Aside from the infant, her kids are only five and three).

She told me, "I do make that much, because the kids gobble it up. Then I'll eat it for lunch during the week."

"I can't believe your kids eat fish!!"

"Yup! It all started from this recipe."

2 red peppers, *cut into thick slices*

1 lb salmon, *cut into chunks*

1 lb sole, flounder, OR tilapia, *cut into chunks*

2 tsp salt, *divided*

¼ tsp black pepper, *divided*

1 tsp garlic powder, *divided*

1 tsp smoked paprika, *divided*

1 tsp cumin

8 garlic cloves, *crushed*

¼ cup fresh cilantro, *chopped*

2 Tbsp tomato paste

pinch crushed red pepper
(or more if you like it hotter)

> calories
> 185 calories per serving
>
> shani taub exchange
> 2 proteins per serving

[1]   Line a sauté pan with red pepper slices. Top with fish; season with half the salt, pepper, garlic powder, smoked paprika, and cumin. Add all the fresh garlic and cilantro.

[2]   Whisk together 1 cup boiling water, tomato paste, remaining salt, pepper, garlic powder, smoked paprika, cumin, and the crushed red pepper. Pour liquid over fish; bring to a boil over medium-high heat.

[3]   Cover pan; reduce heat and simmer for 45 minutes, until fish is cooked through and there is still some liquid left in the pan. Serve fish with pan sauce.

Real Life Branzino

Yields 2 servings (2 fillets per person)   ▫   Pareve

During the photo shoots for this book, we'd often order the fish fresh for delivery. At the same time, Esti would order fish for her family's dinner. That would often include crispy fish for the kids and branzino fillets for the adults. One day, when we were running a little later than usual, Esti roasted her branzino in the studio's kitchen and told me to taste it. I admit, I was surprised something so simple that takes 30 seconds to prep could be so good! I told Esti that, to me, this recipe is so "real life." Hence the name. This recipe also works great using barramundi.

4 branzino fillets, *with or without skin*

1 lemon, *halved*

2 garlic cloves, *crushed*

¼ tsp **paprika**

¼ tsp **dried basil**

¼ tsp **salt**

pinch **coarse black pepper**

calories
110 calories per fillet,
220 calories per serving

shani taub exchange
1 protein per fillet

[1]   Preheat oven to 450°F. Line a baking sheet with parchment paper; coat with nonstick cooking spray.

[2]   Place branzino fillets onto prepared baking sheet. Squeeze juice from lemon halves over branzino. Sprinkle with garlic, paprika, basil, salt, and pepper. Bake for 9-10 minutes.

Quinoa-Stuffed Branzino

Yields 4 servings ▫ Pareve

Whole branzino is often served stuffed, but there's no way I'm getting near a fish if the bones and eyeballs are still attached. Chaya Raskin, of Raskin's Fish, has been the source of lots of my fish tips over the last couple of years. Chaya also taught me that I could order branzino "butterflied," which she says is "a technique used to open up the fish and remove the bones, ideal for stuffing." The result is a beautiful one-dish meal with an impressive presentation and great variety of flavors.

1 Tbsp oil

2 red peppers, *sliced*

2 small fennel bulbs, *sliced*

2 whole branzino fillets (about 2 lb total)**,** *butterflied*

salt, *for sprinkling*

coarse black pepper, *for sprinkling*

1 lemon, *quartered, for garnish*

STUFFING

1 cup cooked quinoa

½ red pepper, *thinly sliced*

½ zucchini, *finely diced*

2 Tbsp golden raisins

½ tsp garlic powder

1½ tsp salt

pinch coarse black pepper

calories
280 calories per serving

shani taub exchange
1 protein, ½ bread,
½ vegetable, ¼ fat,
¼ fruit per serving

[1] Preheat oven to 400°F. Add oil to a baking pan; top with sliced red peppers and fennel. Bake for 20 minutes, or until soft.

[2] **Meanwhile, prepare the stuffing:** In a bowl, combine cooked quinoa, red pepper, zucchini, raisins, garlic powder, salt, and pepper.

[3] Place the butterflied fillets onto the peppers and fennel. Season the inner surfaces of the fish with salt and pepper. Divide the quinoa mixture between the 2 fillets; fold the two sides together (there's no need for cooking twine as once the fish is cooked, it will hold its shape). Sprinkle the outside of the fish with additional salt and pepper; coat with nonstick cooking spray (or use 1 additional tablespoon oil to coat).

[4] Using a sharp knife, make 3 diagonal slashes on the upper side of the fish (do not cut all the way through). This will help you slice the fish for serving after it has cooked. Bake for 25 minutes.

[5] Once fish is cool enough to handle, transfer stuffed fillets to a platter; top with red pepper/ fennel mixture. The best way to do this is with gloved hands. Serve with fresh lemon.

I don't really believe in diet desserts. Desserts, I feel, were meant to be enjoyed in small portions on special occasions. Most of these, though, just happen to be light and are the perfect "something sweet" items you need on a Friday night or another time. Though I used sweeteners to cut calories when possible, they're still wholesome options even if you prefer to use sugar. -Victoria

Desserts
(and sweet & salty treats)

I think the best desserts are a weight loss ... we enjoy the taste of that success longer than anything else that's sweet. But we're all human, and we all need to have our treats once in a while. When we're entertaining, we can enjoy dessert along with our company, and these recipes were designed so we could enjoy both the sweets and the weight loss. -Shani

Mixed Berry Fruit Gelee

Yields 8 servings ▫ Pareve
Gluten-Free ▫ Sugar-Free ▫ Low Carb

This is my favorite dessert right now (the reason I have 12 pounds of frozen fruit in my freezer?). Since when can a jelled dessert be so elegant? And actually healthy? My ice cream is getting very jealous.

1 *(16-oz)* **bag frozen strawberries,** *completely thawed*

1 *(16-oz)* **bag frozen blueberries,** *completely thawed*

2 *(3-oz)* **boxes sugar-free strawberry OR raspberry jell powder**

½ cup fresh blueberries, chopped strawberries, pomegranate seeds, OR fruit of your choice

calories
49 calories per serving

shani taub exchange
1 fruit

[1] Add thawed strawberries and blueberries to the jar of a blender or food processor. Blend until smooth. You should have 3-4 cups puree.

[2] Add puree to a saucepan over medium-high heat. Bring to a boil. Turn off heat and stir in jell powder.

[3] Divide mixture between dessert glasses. Refrigerate until set.

[4] Top gelees with fruit of choice. Keep refrigerated until ready to serve.

[Try This!] For a lighter, calorie-free dessert with more flavor complexity, omit the fruit puree and prepare your jel powder with berry-flavored tea.

[Shani Says] This is the perfect Friday night dessert!

Lemon Meringue Napoleon

Yields 12 servings □ Pareve

Do you want a dessert that's crunchy, creamy, sweet, refreshing, and made with (yup!) real sugar?!? There are no dessert compromises here ... just naturally light components joining together in one satisfying sweet that everyone around the table can enjoy together.

WONTON CRISPS

24 wonton wrappers   **cinnamon,** *for sprinkling*
2 tsp sugar

LOW-FAT LEMON CURD

10 Tbsp sugar   **zest of 1 lemon**
⅔ cup lemon juice   **2 eggs**

COOKED MERINGUE

½ cup sugar   **3 egg whites**
¼ cup water   **¼ tsp cream of tartar**

berries of your choice

calories
129 calories per serving

shani taub exchange
N/A

[1] Preheat oven to 350°F. Line 2 baking sheets with parchment paper. Add wonton wrappers; sprinkle with sugar and cinnamon. Bake until golden and crisp, 7-8 minutes.

[2] **Meanwhile, prepare the curd:** Add sugar, lemon juice, and lemon zest to a small saucepan. Bring to a boil to dissolve sugar. Add eggs to a bowl and slowly pour in the lemon mixture, whisking quickly as you pour. Return mixture to the saucepan and cook until thickened, about 2 minutes. Set aside.

[3] **Prepare the meringue:** Combine sugar and water in a small saucepan. Bring to a boil; boil for 4 minutes.

[4] Meanwhile, combine egg whites and cream of tartar in the bowl of an electric mixer. Beat until soft peaks form.

[5] With the mixer on high speed, very slowly pour hot sugar liquid into meringue. After pouring in the sugar, beat meringue for 7 minutes.

[6] **To assemble:** Top a wonton crisp with a spoonful lemon curd, ¼ cup meringue, and berries. Top with a second wonton crisp; serve immediately.

[Try This!] You can also serve this mousse-style, by combining the meringue and curd in a dessert glass. Use the wonton crisps and berries as garnish.

[Make Ahead] The wonton crisps and lemon curd can be prepared ahead. Meringue must be prepared fresh shortly before serving. You can also assemble curd and meringue in cups and freeze; add fruit and crisps before serving.

[Shani Says] Save this as a maintenance treat to enjoy along with your guests when you're entertaining and want a light dessert that everyone can appreciate.

Creme Brulee

Yields 14 (4-ounce) creme brulees □ Dairy
Gluten-Free □ Low Carb

This is the only recipe in this book where I use just yolks instead of whites (I'm sure you'll find lots of uses for those whites). Now here's why it belongs in this book: Traditional creme brulee is made with heavy cream, at 820 calories a cup. My challenge? To duplicate it using whole milk, at 150 calories a cup. Is it even possible? Yes! We now have a 115-calorie cup of sweet, rich satisfaction.

4 cups whole milk, *divided*

1 tsp pure vanilla extract OR vanilla bean paste OR 1 vanilla bean, *scraped*

4 Tbsp sugar

6 egg yolks

1 *(approx. 1.7-oz)* **package sugar-free instant vanilla pudding mix**

1 Tbsp cornstarch

turbinado sugar *(Sugar in the Raw), for sprinkling*

calories
115 calories per serving

shani taub exchange
N/A

[1] Preheat oven to 325°F.

[2] In a saucepan, combine 2 cups milk, vanilla, and sugar over medium-low heat. Bring barely to a simmer.

[3] In a mixing bowl, using a large wire whisk, whisk together remaining 2 cups milk, egg yolks, pudding powder, and cornstarch. Whisk until completely smooth.

[4] Slowly pour warm milk into egg mixture, whisking as you pour. Whisk until smooth. Strain if desired.

[5] Return mixture to saucepan; cook until slightly thickened, about 4 additional minutes.

[6] **Prepare the water bath:** Place a large baking pan on the middle rack of the oven. Add hot water and ramekins until the hot water comes halfway up the sides of the ramekins. Transfer creme brulee mixture to a measuring cup (for easier pouring); divide between ramekins.

[7] Bake for 45 minutes, until creme brulee seems almost set. Remove from oven, let cool, and chill in the refrigerator overnight.

[8] Before serving, sprinkle each creme brulee with 1 teaspoon turbinado sugar. Use a kitchen torch to melt the sugar before serving.

[Make Ahead] You can make creme brulee up to 1 week ahead and keep refrigerated. Torch it just before serving.

[Shani Says] When my clients move onto the maintenance program, I allow them a 100-calorie treat of any type per day. This would be considered that daily treat.

Chocolate Brownies

Yields 12 servings   ▫   Pareve

Fat-free baking is a funny and quirky thing (and there's definitely loads and loads more trial and error than with traditional baking!). Usually, fat-free baked goods are loaded with sugar. I think it's fascinating that a sweet potato can both replace the fat in a traditional chocolate cake ... and contribute enough sweetness to keep this cake super low in sugar too.

¼ cup cocoa	pinch salt
1 tsp espresso powder OR instant coffee granules	4 *(6-oz)* jars sweet potato baby food
¼ cup sugar	3 eggs
½ cup flour	2 tsp vanilla
1½ tsp baking soda	3 oz bittersweet chocolate, *chopped*

calories
119 calories per serving

shani taub exchange
1 bread

[1] Preheat oven to 350°F. Coat a 9- x 13-inch baking pan with nonstick cooking spray.

[2] In a large bowl, whisk together cocoa, espresso powder, sugar, flour, baking soda, and salt (you can also do this directly in the baking pan!).

[3] In a cup or bowl, whisk together sweet potato puree, eggs, and vanilla. Combine with dry ingredients.

[4] Melt chocolate (or leave chocolate unmelted for crunchy bits in the brownie). Fold into batter.

[5] Pour batter into prepared baking pan; bake for 30 minutes. Let cool; cut into 12 large squares.

[Good to Know] For a cake-like consistency, use fresh sweet potatoes instead of baby food. Roast a 1-pound sweet potato at 400°F until very soft, about 1 hour. Peel (yielding ¾ pound sweet potato flesh) and puree until smooth.

[For the Family] Besides being light, this may be the sneakiest way to serve veggies to kids!

[Make Ahead] These can be frozen, but don't eat them straight from the freezer. Let them thaw for best taste and texture.

[Shani Says] Enjoy this as Shabbos morning breakfast.

Peanut Butter Milkshake

Yields 1 shake □ Dairy
Gluten-Free □ Sugar-Free □ Low Carb

It was a summer afternoon, and I really had a craving for ice cream. While I was deciding whether or not to go to the ice cream store, I decided to test this shake concept that had been in my mind ... and that ice cream craving was satiated.

4-6 ice cubes
¾ cup lowfat milk
2 Tbsp peanut butter powder
(such as PB2 or PBFit)

1 Tbsp sugar-free vanilla pudding powder
½ tsp vanilla
2-3 packets sweetener

calories
165 calories

shani taub exchange
2 proteins

□ Place all ingredients into a blender. Blend to combine. Serve immediately.

Peanut Butter Cups

Yields 12 cups □ Pareve

That after-dinner sweet for those who need their chocolate and peanut butter.

½ cup PLUS 2 Tbsp sugar-free *(or regular)* **chocolate chips,** *divided*
½ cup peanut butter powder
(such as PB2 or PBFit)
5 Tbsp water

4 packets sweetener
¼ cup Rice Krispies OR Reese's cereal, *crushed*
1 Tbsp milk or soy milk

calories
59 calories per cup
(84 calories with regular chocolate chips)

shani taub exchange
N/A

[1] Preheat oven to 250°F. Line a mini muffin pan with mini cupcake liners. Spoon 1 teaspoon chocolate chips into each cup. Bake for 5-6 minutes to melt chocolate.

[2] Meanwhile, in a small bowl, combine peanut butter powder, water, sweetener, and crushed cereal.

[3] Melt remaining chocolate chips with milk in the microwave for 30 seconds. Stir until smooth.

[4] Using a mini spoon, flatten the melted chocolate in each muffin cup. Divide peanut butter filling between cups. Use the mini spoon to top filling with melted chocolate. Freeze until firm.

[Good to Know] We found that Lily's stevia-sweetened dark chocolate chips were the sugar-free chips that tasted most like regular.

Citrus Cheesecake

Yields 10 mini cheesecakes　▫　Dairy
Gluten-Free　▫　Low Carb

When Leah and I first published the "180-Calorie Cheesecake" in Dairy Made Easy, it was a cheesecake game changer. Why cut a 600-calorie slice when the 180-calorie version was seriously just as good? This time, I omitted the crust and added a refreshing citrus topping for an even lighter version.

1½ cups light vanilla Greek yogurt
2 eggs
2 Tbsp sugar

1 tsp vanilla
1 Tbsp cornstarch
zest of 1 orange

TOPPING
½ cup orange juice
1 Tbsp sugar-free jell powder

5-7 kumquats,
sliced into thin rounds

calories
54 calories
per cheesecake

shani taub exchange
2 cheesecakes =
1 protein

[1]　Preheat oven to 350°F. Coat a mini cheesecake or muffin pan well with nonstick cooking spray.

[2]　In a blender, combine yogurt, eggs, sugar, vanilla, cornstarch, and orange zest. Pour into prepared pan; bake for 20 minutes.

[3]　**Prepare the topping:** In a small saucepan, bring orange juice to a boil; whisk in jell powder. Let sit until mixture solidifies but is still pourable.

[4]　Spoon some of the mixture onto cheesecakes. Add kumquat slices. Jell will continue to solidify as it cools. Keep refrigerated until ready to serve.

Bread Pudding Two Ways

Yields 6 servings   □   Dairy or Pareve
Gluten-Free   □   Sugar Free

I enjoy dessert after a restaurant meal on a special occasion. And while many people order the standards — i.e., the ubiquitous lava cake — I like to look for the unique options on the menu. It was on one such night that I enjoyed a warm, nut-studded banana bread pudding. Everyone else at the table abandoned their typical desserts to grab bites of mine; the consensus was that it was the best dessert of the night ... inspiring me to create a light version. Even if you enjoy this with sugar instead of a substitute, it's still a wholesome option, with a quarter of the calories of that tired lava cake.

1 egg

⅓ cup granulated Splenda

¼ cup milk or soymilk

½ tsp cinnamon

3 slices 60-calorie whole wheat bread, *cut into cubes*

FOR BANANA-NUT VERSION

1 cup mashed banana *(2 bananas)*   **2 Tbsp chopped pecans**

FOR APPLE-RAISIN VERSION

1 cup unsweetened applesauce   **1 Tbsp raisins**

1 small apple, *diced*

> calories
> 95 calories per serving for banana;
> 81 calories per serving for apple
> ----------
> shani taub exchange
> 1 bread per serving

[1] Preheat oven to 350°F.

[2] In a bowl, whisk together egg, Splenda, milk, cinnamon, and mashed banana or applesauce. Add bread cubes; stir well to combine.

[3] For apple version, fold in diced apple and raisins.

[4] Divide mixture between 6 ramekins.

[5] For banana version, sprinkle with 1 teaspoon chopped pecans.

[6] Bake for 20 minutes, until puddings are set and golden on top. Enjoy warm.

[Shani Says] Fruits are high in carbs, so sometimes it's fine to interchange them with your bread servings.

Pumpkin Pie

Yields 3 servings   □   Dairy or Pareve
Gluten-Free   □   Sugar-Free   □   Low Carb

Here's what I love about these little crustless pies. Besides satisfying that need for something sweet after a meal, these are also really filling. Pumpkin is high in fiber, low in calories, and unlike most desserts, actually has nutritional value. Don't want to wait until these bake? Simply pull out your puree and whisk in the sweetener of your choice and some spice. A spoon or two of sugar-free instant vanilla pudding powder will also help add creaminess to your no-bake version.

1 *(15-oz)* **can pure pumpkin puree**
(not pumpkin pie filling)
½ cup milk or soy milk

2 eggs

⅔ cup granulated Splenda
1 tsp cinnamon OR pumpkin pie spice

calories
114 calories per pie

shani taub exchange
1 bread, 1 protein

[1] Preheat oven to 350°F.

[2] In a bowl, whisk together pumpkin puree, milk, eggs, Splenda, and cinnamon.

[3] Pour mixture into mini pie pans or ramekins. Bake until set, 25-30 minutes.

[Shani Says] Pumpkin is one of those ingredients where you get so much quantity and nutrients for the calories ... and it's so creamy! Each of these pies is a very generous size.

Mango Sorbet

Yields 3 servings ◻ Pareve

Frozen fruit is naturally super sweet, as it's frozen at peak ripeness, making this satisfyingly sweet, even without any added sweetener ... and it's creamy too! Though you can create any flavor of sugar-free sorbet using this technique, mango, coconut, and lime are especially magical together.

2 cups frozen mango cubes   **2 Tbsp lime juice**
¼ cup light coconut milk

> calories
> 78 calories per serving
> ----
> shani taub exchange
> 1 fruit

[1] In a blender, combine mango, coconut milk, and lime juice.

[2] Serve immediately or store in freezer. If freezing, thaw before scooping.

[Shani Says] Eat this with a baby spoon ...
it will last a long time; savor each bite.

Pomegranate Granita

Yields 4 servings ◻ Pareve

Another feel-good, super flavorful, and refreshing treat.

2 cups pomegranate juice   **¼ cup lime juice**
¼ cup granulated Splenda

> calories
> 78 calories per serving
> ----
> shani taub exchange
> 1 fruit

[1] Combine pomegranate juice, Splenda, and lime juice in a baking pan. Freeze for 1 hour. Run a fork through the ice to scrape any frozen bits. Return to freezer.

[2] Once frozen, use a fork to scrape the ice again and serve. You can also freeze the mixture completely and simply let thaw a bit before scraping and serving.